FAMILY ARRESTED

How To Survive
The Incarceration Of A Loved One

Ann Edenfield

PUBLISHER'S CATALOGING-IN-PUBLICATION

Edenfield, Ann.
 Family arrested: how to survive the incarceration of
a loved one / Ann Edenfield. -- 1st ed.
 p. cm.
 Includes index.
 ISBN 1-58943-060-3

 1. Prisoners' families--Effect of imprisonment on--
United States. 2. Prisoners--United States--Family
relationships. I. Title.

 HV8886.U5E34 2002   362.7
                QBI02-701795

PUBLISHER'S NOTE

Americana Publishing, Inc.
303 San Mateo NE, Suite 104 A
Albuquerque, NM 87108

Praise for *Family Arrested: How To Survive The Incarceration Of A Loved One*

"Although the focus of her information is to help those victims, her book is a must read for anyone who truly desires to understand the full meaning of incarceration."
—Eloy L. Mondragon, Former NM Secretary of Corrections

"Ann Edenfield is to be commended for shining a little light on an otherwise darkened corner of American society."
—William Harmening, IL Securities Department

"So readable and so honest... I could sit at Ms. Edenfield's feet and learn a lot."
—Ginger Newlin, Licensed Clinical Social Worker

"Practical, non-judgmental, and incredibly helpful...fills a huge void in the marketplace."
—Traci Cothran, Audio Book World

"A book without equal."
—John Charles, Crystal Cathedral Ministries

"Even though I am an attorney, *Family Arrested* taught me many things about the prison system and how families can cope with what is an extremely traumatic situation."
—Tom Smidt, Attorney

"A story of faithfulness and perseverance that bolsters courage and offers hope. Ann Edenfield shares her story in ways that may help us examine our own attitudes of rejection or compassion."
—The Rev. Dr. Randall Webb, Global LOGOS

"A moving account of a wife and mother whose faith was unswerving in her determination to help her family survive the stigma of incarceration."
—Homer Gonzales, NM Corrections Department

"Could be used as a tool by the courts and to orient folks to the upheaval of an arrest."
—Rick Stoff, Audio Publishers Association

"A handbook of life inside or outside a prison."
—Alvin Cooperman, Emmy award winning producer

"A must read for corrections administrators, criminal justice students, and the families of defendants who are facing incarceration. In my 33 years in law enforcement I never considered what had to be faced by the other victim of most crimes—the family of the prisoner."
—Lou Campanozi, Retired Police Chief

"Provides a wealth of information that should prove invaluable for individuals facing circumstances similar to Ms. Edenfield's."
—Greg Thornton, Moody Press

"As gripping as a novel...I think all parents would benefit from the suggestions."
—Sandy Bishop, American Bible Society

"Filled with practical suggestions and coping strategies..."
—Jim Mustin, Family and Corrections Network

"Edenfield not only gives families the tools and guidance they need to cope and rebuild their lives, but also offers a challenge to communities, institutions, and congregations about how they can be sources of help, hope, and healing for spouses and children, who are too often shunned or forgotten in their time of greatest need."
—Eugene C. Roehlkepartain, Search Institute

Acknowledgements

There are many people to thank for assisting me with this book, for encouraging me over the years, and for standing by me through the darkest days of my life. I have discovered true friendship in so many, and I am blessed to have so many people in my life that care about my sons and me. I also have come to believe that friends are quiet angels who lift us to our feet when our wings have trouble remembering how to fly.

The angels to thank are many. First, I would like to thank my mom for her unfaltering support throughout my life. She has always been by my side, encouraging me and supporting me through her love and financial support. She has been the finest role model a daughter could ever ask for. My brother and sister-in-law provided financial support to me, and I hope that some-day I can show my love to others as they have shown their love to me.

I would also like to thank my in-laws for their incredible emotional and financial help during my husband's incarceration and over the years. And, special thanks to Olga Wilson for her many years of love and devotion to our family. I am also grate-ful to Friedje vanGils and the staff at Escuela del Sol Montessori for their unconditional love, support, and fine education that they provided to my sons.

The Rev. Dr. David Poling, my pastor, mentor, and friend will be forever held dear to my heart. He believed in me from our first meeting, trusted me to work with the youth in his church, and always offered words of support and prayer.

The Rev. Dr. Dale K. Milligan (b.1925 - d.1998), founder of the LOGOS System Associates, helped me discover my gifts and welcomed me unconditionally into LSA. He was my pastor, mentor, and friend. I would like to thank The Rev. Dr. Randall Webb, President of Global LOGOS and former fellow LOGOS System Associate staff member and Global Ministry Director, for his confidence in me. His counsel guided my vision of the ministry that was taking place in Russia, India, and around the United States.

There are hundreds of friends/volunteers that have believed in the Wings Ministry and have helped it to continue and grow. Special thanks to Jori and Tim Bowen, Karen Bramlitt, Rev. Ann Burgdorf, Don Conklin, Caroline Crawford, Rev. Daniel Erdman, Debbie Foster, Mary Lou and Miguel Gonzales, Joy and Tom Hayes, Beverly and Bill Lackey, Tracey, Tim, Sarah, and John Meisenheimer, Jim and Ann Mogford, Jenny and Bob Mueller, Cathy and Lisa Pfefferle, Alf Reeb, Jack Reneau, Rev. Byron Rogers, Rev. Randy Webb, and Pat Woldt.

Thank you to Jim Zanios, American Bible Society, Gideons, and Guideposts Magazine for all their contributions to Wings over the years.

Special thanks to Debbie Foster, Marty Brown, Karen Bramlitt, Doris Milligan, Tom Smidt, Charles Daniels, Eloy Mondragon, and Cel Vigil for reading my manuscript. And, thanks to Lesley Poling-Kempes for all her editorial help from twelve years ago and Zack Clem for his support of this book.

I especially appreciate my editor, Lisa Savard, who is not only a co-worker, but a friend. She thoughtfully and profession-ally edited my words into this finished book. Thank you, Lisa!

George Lovato, Jr., CEO of Americana Publishing, Inc., has been an amazing colleague and visionary. He trusted me to help build his vision, Americana Publishing, Inc. From my first meeting with him, he expressed the need for a book like this and encouraged me to do my best.

And, lastly, I would like to thank and dedicate this book to my four sons—the joys of my life. They are what kept me going in times of struggle, and they continually bring sunshine into my life while growing into fine, young men. I am proud to be their mother, and I thank them for their understanding and love throughout our journey together.

Disclaimer

This book offers advice based on my personal experience with the United States legal and prison system. This story is written from my perspective—the wife of an inmate. I am not an attorney; therefore, this book cannot and does not attempt to take the place of an attorney. Please consult with an attorney for all legal matters pertaining to your loved one's court case, trial, and incarceration.

This book addresses the prisoner's family and the common issues they face, whether their loved one is in a federal or state prison. Each state has its own guidelines, rules, and procedures, and this book is to be used only as a general guide. Based on current incarceration rates, 2002 Bureau of Justice statistics report that one out of every twenty Americans will be in state or federal prison sometime during his or her lifetime. These figures are staggering! This book was written for the millions of us that experience the issues surrounding incarceration without any understanding of the justice system.

My husband was in a federal prison. Therefore, all of my personal experiences come from the federal prison system. However, I have tried to be as accurate as possible, offering suggestions and guidelines that apply to both the federal and state penal systems by consulting with experts in different state and the federal prisons. Yet, bear in mind that rules and regulations constantly change. When you need specific information about a particular subject, check with your lawyer, the inmate, the courts, or the institution. Each institution should have an Inmate Handbook. I suggest that you get a copy of this handbook in order to understand the policies pertaining to the institution where your loved one is incarcerated.

For the ease of writing, I am using "he" when describing the inmate. Statistics regarding prison population reveal that the majority of all inmates are male. Therefore, the majority of you reading this book will be relating to male inmates. Obviously, she may be interchanged with he.

Forward

This first person account on how to deal with the arrest, trial, and imprisonment of a husband and father is unique in the publishing annals. *Family Arrested* is written for the thousands of people struggling with the criminal event of a loved one and the imprisonment which follows. This book describes all the confusing steps that families face approaching arrest, bond, trial, sentencing, and incarceration.

With over six million people in prison, on parole or probation, or awaiting trial, twenty to thirty million others are directly affected. The toll on spouses, children, and extended family is staggering. Ann Edenfield shares all the emotions and intimate details that accompany such a damaging sentence—not her husband's, but her trama.

A widely ignored sector of this country comes to light in this book by a determined and gifted woman. Suddenly, she is a single parent raising four sons on $9,000.00 a year and driving five hundred miles round trip for prison visits. Her coping skills ignite as she shops flea markets, buys day old bread, and clothes her family in thrift shop bargains.

Edenfield carefully probes the dynamics of prison families as they interact with neighborhood suspicion, classroom taunts, and community ostracism. She provides tested strategies for building self-esteem in spouses and children who have been stricken by a parent's imprisonment.

Why is this a first time book and why haven't other writers dealt with this serious social condition? Primarily, there is so much guilt, shame, depression, and social stigma surrounding crime that few people have ever been willing to tell their story. As spouses and children alternate between denial and distance from these painful circumstances, the motivation to relive such moral failure and restimulate public scorn is not going to happen. Next, the criminal justice system is so massively bureaucratic that even those on the inside have a daily challenge to interpret its function and adapt to its multiple changes. Ann Edenfield provides a workable roadmap for beginners.

Most importantly, the author has the insight and nerve to go beyond her private "arrest" at home and bring positive, immediate help to thousands of others. In many ways this is a woman's book, for other wives and their children. Yet, the counsel for inmate husbands and loved ones is just as direct and just as helpful. Ultimately, this book is filled with hope and surprising triumph. It will generate immediate help to those in need and to the many that serve them.

—The Rev. Dr. David Poling
Sea of Glory
Co-author, Ken Wales

Table of Contents

We don't receive wisdom; we must discover it for ourselves after a journey that no one can take for us or spare us.

—Marcel Proust

Prologue

Studies show that only death causes more stress on a family than the incarceration of a loved one. Yet, there is very little help available to the families of prison inmates. Therefore, this book is offered as a self-help guide for those who find themselves involved with our country's criminal justice system.

Just after the birth of my fourth son, my husband was given a fifteen year sentence in a federal prison. Following my husband's imprisonment, I searched for books and materials that would help my family and me deal with the trauma that his arrest and imprisonment imposed on our lives. Surviving the incarceration of a loved one is not something anyone ever wants to be an expert on, but I felt it would be better to know what the challenges were rather than feel victimized by the legal system and prison system that had become a part of my family's lives. I searched the database of a major university library, which yielded two articles that addressed the problems experienced by the families of death row inmates. Instead of finding information, I found a void. I felt as if my problem was so trivial that it did not warrant explanation. But I knew differently. I was facing the most difficult and stressful time of my life and I needed a lifeline, even if it meant making one for myself.

In my quest for knowledge, I sought out the Dean of a university psychology department and explained that I was searching for literature to help guide me through the maze of legal and emotional challenges that greeted me daily since my husband's arrest. Although the psychology professor knew of studies about prisoners, he could not find any resources in his library addressing the legal and personal problems of prisoners' wives and families. The only book the professor found that was even remotely related to my dilemma was a Norwegian study of fishermen's children, and the impact that a father's nine month absence had on the children's lives. But my children and I were facing a fifteen year separation from their father. Needless to say, I found the Norwegian study useless. That afternoon in the professor's office marked the beginning of the research, interviews, and general soul searching that resulted in this book.

I now understand why only the death of a loved one causes more stress on a family member than the arrest, trial, and imprisonment of a loved one. In many ways, the state of mind is very similar to that of widower's. The shock, grief, anger, and loneliness experienced by a widower are often the same emotions experienced by the spouse of a prisoner.

If someone you love is facing arrest, trial, and a probable prison sentence, it is imperative that you, your family, and friends prepare for the emotional and financial upheaval that go hand in hand with incarceration and involvement in our country's criminal justice system. This book deals primarily with the dilemmas faced by the wives of inmates—those women whom I describe as "arrested" and struggling within the confines of emotional, social, and financial imprisonment. However, the information is also applicable to the families and friends of prisoners.

Knowledge of the pitfalls and dead ends that lie ahead does not insure avoidance of them; but, as I learned during my own long years of my spouse's incarceration, education and knowledge help minimize feelings of helplessness and fear. Therefore, I suggest educating yourself. Face your predicament head on. Your familiarity with the legal and social systems you and your imprisoned loved one are now involved in is your greatest tool for survival and growth.

The title, *Family Arrested*, describes my experience completely, because, in essence, our whole family was arrested. We were stopped in our tracks. We weren't handcuffed and hauled off to prison, but our whole family structure was thrown into chaos. My husband's incarceration affected all of us in very significant ways. My family was suddenly ostracized from much of what we had known and counted on. It felt like we had invisible bars surrounding us, and many people, including friends, did not want to get near us. We were a *Family Arrested*.

Arrest. Trial. Conviction.

stage

I

There is no chance, no destiny, no fate that can circumvent or hinder or control the firm resolve of a determined soul.

—Ella Wheeler Wilcox

1

The Arrest

"Miss Ann, Miss Ann, the phone!" cried out our ordinarily calm Jamaican housekeeper. I immediately knew by the tone in her voice that something was wrong. Up until that moment, it had been a routinely chaotic, summer morning. I was sitting at the kitchen table amidst boxes of cereal breast-feeding my eight-month-old baby, while my three young boys hollered above the din of the contractor's hammering and made a general mess of their breakfast. Instead of rushing off to our real estate office with my husband, I was delayed with the baby's feeding, which was taking longer than usual. And, while making the time to ensure the contractor and his men were on course for the addition to our house, I had told my husband to go to the office and I would catch up with him later. Although the house was in general disarray, the sight of my boys, ages eight, six, two, and eight months, reassured me of all the blessings in my life.

And then I picked up the phone. In a trembling voice,

our nearly hysterical secretary described the scene that had just unfolded before her eyes. FBI agents had come to the office, taken my husband outside to the parking lot, thrown him down on the pavement, and handcuffed him before roughly pushing him into their car. She was panic-stricken. I tried to calm her down, but I was quickly reaching levels of hysteria. A million questions raced through my mind. *Arrested? How could it be? What did this mean? What should I do?* I knew I needed to stay level-headed. I tried to get details from her while telling her everything was going to be all right. I assured her that it must be a mistake.

During the two weeks that preceded my horror, my husband had received threatening warnings that he could be linked to some of his acquaintances, who had recently been indicted in Pennsylvania on drug trafficking charges. Although that news caused a dark cloud to hover over my thoughts, I doubted the reality of such threats. I didn't think it could happen to us. We had a thriving real estate firm, a beautiful house on several acres of premier property, good standing in our community and church, and four beautiful sons. We had it all. Even after my husband retained a criminal attorney, we continued to live our lives as if the threat of indictment was not there. In hindsight, I wish we would have reorganized our lives to prepare for the possibility of arrest—complete obliteration of life as we knew it.

After calming the secretary, I hung up the phone and raced to the phone in my bedroom, which allowed me the privacy I needed to speak to my husband's lawyer. I rapidly explained the situation regarding my husband. He, too, was surprised. He thought that if an indictment had been issued, he would have been the first to be notified. The excuses given later to him by the authorities were that they were afraid my husband might run; therefore, a surprise arrest ensured a successful capture. He assured me that he would handle everything. He would call the detention center, find out about charges, bail, and all the details of the case. He talked and I listened. He was very kind and I had complete confidence in him. But when our conversation was over, I could barely hang up the phone. I was numb. I couldn't move. The gnawing pain inside my soul told me that my life would never be the same again. *Arrested!* My mind flooded with thoughts of newspaper headlines and TV and radio news clips, and I wondered what people would say. I did not cry, yell, or even move. It was as if my body had died, my heart barely pumping. It was August 5, 1986, and my husband was arrested and charged with conspiracy to import illegal drugs into the U.S.

When I finally gathered my wits, I realized I needed to call my in-laws. However, I had to be careful how I spoke to them since my father-in-law already had two heart bypass operations; I feared that this terrible news could endanger his health. Nevertheless, I made the call and requested they both pick up a phone to hear what I had to say. I explained that everything was under control, but their son had been arrested and charged with conspiracy to import illegal drugs. We had not forewarned them about any of the possibilities regarding this matter, so they were shocked. I was trying my best to be calm and not alarm them, but when the news sunk in and they realized my fragile state, they relayed comforting words and offered their support. It was such a relief that they didn't disown us after hearing the terrible truth of their son's arrest. Rather, they cared and didn't desert us. I had now shared my living nightmare with loving people. In that moment, I felt slightly strengthened. We finally said our good-byes, and as I placed the receiver down, I collapsed into the fetal position. I started crying; my whole being ached. Suddenly, I had never been so frightened or felt so alone in my life.

I don't know how much time passed, but I eventually forced myself to get up and face the world. I explained the story to the housekeeper, and then told the boys that their daddy would not be home that night. Since they were used to his traveling, they were not concerned by the news. However, I didn't tell them any of the details of the arrest, because I had to be strong for them. In fact, I was so distraught that I was afraid I would collapse again if I told them anymore. To a group of shocked faces, I told the contractors what had just happened and they offered support. Suddenly, the work on the house seemed so insignificant, and I knew I had to stop it. I told the men to take the day off and that I would call them later and let them know what the arrest meant regarding future construction. They packed up some tools and left.

The rest of the day was agonizingly slow, and I could barely function. My body moved, but my mind was blank and lifeless. I fed the boys, cooked and cleaned, but all I could think of was the arrest. My husband's lawyer kept me well informed about what was happening. He thought there would be no problem with bail and that perhaps my husband would be home the next day. Since he was handling everything, it seemed as if there was no reason for me to go down to the jail.

In retrospect, it felt like a day when someone had died. There was not only the sudden shock of the arrest, but there was shame, embarrassment, and the total uncertainty of my family's future to deal with. I had made calls to a few family members and close friends, but I functioned in a daze of fear. Instinctively, I knew that August 5, 1986, would be a day that I would never forget. No matter how hard I tried, life couldn't be the same for any of us.

My husband's lawyer called around 9:00 PM the night of the arrest, warning me that government agents would be searching my home the next day. To help ease my fears, he told me he would be there with me. As much as he had tried to comfort me, this became one of the most trying experiences for me throughout the entire legal process. My in-laws appeared at my home early the next morning to get my three older sons. My boys were very confused about the last twenty-four hours of activity, so I explained that their daddy had some problems with the law and might be gone for a few days. I could not bear to tell them he was arrested, behind bars, and may not come home for a long time. Fortunately, their excitement over spending the day with their grandparents overshadowed the news about their father.

It seemed as if the boys had just left when the agents arrived. My husband's lawyer greeted them at the door. I was introduced to them and they showed me all the legal documents that allowed them to search our house. I knew we had nothing to hide, so I didn't fear they would discover anything out of the ordinary. The whole procedure just frightened me, however, as I had never had dealings with law enforcement authorities until that point. They seemed like decent men, so I treated them like any other guests in my home. They reacted with surprise at my offer of coffee, but accepted it from me. Then my husband's lawyer followed them as they searched every room in our home. It seemed as if I was watching prowlers sifting through my belongings, totally invading my privacy. Yet, they had permission to do so, and there was nothing I could do to stop them. They went through closets and drawers. They read through old love letters, postcards, scraps of paper in my purse, and delved into every square inch of the house. They opened liquor and perfume bottles and poked into my cosmetics. They looked at every picture in every scrapbook and opened boxes that contained childhood mementos. They had pried into the most intimate parts of my family's lives with no regard for my treasured memories or feelings. I felt so violated, as if I had been stripped naked and exposed to the world. Although movies dramatize law enforcement agents tearing down doors to enter a home, pulling naked people out of their bed, and ripping through personal items, the agents in my home acted civil. They tried to put things back in their places, and although boxes were left on the floor, they had not torn or destroyed anything. After hours of searching the house, they took one photo with them. To this day, I believe they were kind to me for two reasons: 1. My husband's lawyer was present; 2. I was polite.

After my husband's lawyer left, I called my in-laws to let them know they could bring the boys back. In the meantime, several neighbors had called to inform me that on the morning of the arrest about twelve cars had been staked out along our dead end road. Later we were told armed agents had also been posted on foot around our property to prevent an escape. I was also informed about front-page headlines in the papers and TV and radio news broadcasts regarding my husband's arrest. The people who called were very kind and offered to help me. But, the countless neighbors and friends that did not call never spoke to me again.

After nine painful days, my husband was finally released on bail. When he returned home to await trial, my family entered the "family arrested" zone: an emotional state of upheaval in which we would live for the next fifteen years. My husband's crime was considered "white collar," but this label did not mean the law was easier on my family than on the families of other accused criminals.

My life, like that of millions of other women, was profoundly affected by my husband's actions. I was not prepared for my new path in life, and I had no understanding of our country's legal system or prison system. The details of a loved one's arrest will vary widely, but one aspect will be the same for everyone: your life will be turned upside down.

The only good is knowledge and the only evil is ignorance.

—Socrates

2

Legal Nuts and Bolts

Indictment

An indictment is the formal accusation presented by a grand jury that charges the person named of a crime. Before a defendant can be convicted, the indictment must be proven beyond a reasonable doubt at trial. However, an indictment is considered probable cause evidence, which satisfies the lower burden of proof. At the federal level, the evidence for an indictment is typically very strong.

Arrest

There is no standard procedure followed by law enforcement agencies to inform you or the accused of a legal problem. Someone caught breaking the law may be immediately arrested, and his family may learn of this arrest via a phone call from the accused or from an attorney. If the accused is the target of a lawsuit, he may simply be notified through the mail. If a grand jury has met and decided to indict the accused, his family could learn of the indictment through the news media, a mailed notice, or a surprise arrest.

The accused may be forewarned of possible legal trouble. If so, he would be wise to contact a lawyer before the arrest. More times than not, however, he may be arrested without warning, and you and your family will find yourselves at the mercy of the judicial system.

If you learn in advance of an impending indictment, contact an attorney. With legal counsel, you may be able to avoid an actual arrest of the accused. However, if arrest is unavoidable, the accused should report to the proper authorities.

While awaiting impending arrest, communication between family members, especially between husband and wife, should be based on honesty. However, it may be difficult for the accused to discuss the details of the alleged crime, particularly immediately after an arrest, since the accused may be feeling considerable shame. The lawyer may have advised the accused not to discuss the case with anyone, including his spouse. This may be very difficult for the family members, but it is also the time to provide as much support to the accused as possible. At some point, the accused must take responsibility for any harm he may have brought on the family, but sometimes that accountability will not take place until much later.

Prepare your family and close friends if arrest is imminent. Children do not have to be told all of the details of a crime in advance of an arrest, but they should be informed of the pending legal problems. If a family member is arrested without warning at your home and in front of young children, remain calm. Do not fight or resist the authorities. The police have been sent to make an arrest and they will perform their job regardless of your reaction. Outrage toward the arresting officers will only make the situation more difficult. Do not add to an already traumatic encounter by striking or resisting an officer. Instead, place your energy into something that can alleviate the conflict. Find an attorney and make bail for your loved one.

The Attorney

Attorney at law, lawyer, or counselor at law are all terms that define a person legally empowered to act as an agent on behalf of another person. An attorney is authorized to perform a variety of civil and criminal legal functions for his client, including drafting legal documents, giving legal advice, and representing his client before courts, administrative agencies, and organizations.

Hiring An Attorney

Hire an attorney with case experience in the type of crime the defendant is accused of. Search for the attorney that is best for your situation and with whom you feel comfortable, because you are going to be spending a lot of time with this person. I recommend that you check with your local state bar association, as they should have information on all the private and public defenders in your state. Martindale-Hubbell generally rates all attorneys, based on peer evaluations, that are in private practice in the United States. In addition, *Best Lawyers in America, 2001-2002,* by Gregory White Smith, should be available for review in most public libraries. This book will not list all attorneys in your area, but the book will list those attorneys most respected by their peers in your area. You can also call the American Bar Association for a list of attorneys who specialize in the defendant's particular legal problem.

Attorneys can be very expensive. In a criminal case, an attorney usually will want most of the fee paid in advance. Because your attorney basically holds your future in his hands, interview and research his credentials as carefully as you would a heart transplant specialist that was going to perform surgery on you or a family member.

Public Defenders

The 6th Amendment of the U.S. Constitution states, "In all criminal prosecutions, the accused shall enjoy the right to a speedy and public trial, by an impartial jury of the State.....and to have the assistance of counsel for his defense." Regardless of the defendant's financial situation, he will be given legal representation. An attorney appointed by the court to represent someone who cannot afford to hire his own attorney is called a public defender—an attorney licensed to practice law in his state. Federal public defender organizations are provided for under federal statutes. In addition to federal public defender programs, most states have (state) public defender organizations.

Public defenders are employed by the state to defend indigent individuals accused of a criminal or felony offense that may result in incarceration. The vast majority of all criminal cases in the United States are handled by public defenders. Do not underestimate their ability and skill. Public defenders are often among the most committed lawyers to be found anywhere.

~Who Is Assigned a Public Defender?

Each court system will determine the financial guidelines that determine whether or not the accused is indigent. Some jurisdictions require tax returns and other documentation as proof that the accused needs a public defender. Other jurisdictions require only the verbal request that the accused needs a public defender. Depending on the actual financial status of the accused, he may be asked to sign a "Contract of Repayment for Services Rendered" by the public defender's office.

~The Limitations of a Public Defender

Depending on his jurisdiction, a public defender will typically have dozens of cases open or active at any one time. For obvious reasons, a public defender must make good use of his time. This does not mean, however, that he will not try to give each client assigned to them his utmost attention and counsel.

You will not have a choice as to the public defender assigned to your case. If the accused speaks a language other than English, a public defender fluent in the appropriate language should be assigned; however, if one is not available, an interpreter will be assigned to the case.

It may be possible to change public defenders if there is a severe personality conflict. But, this can be a burdensome process; therefore, make every effort to cooperate with the attorney assigned to your case.

The public defender accompanies the accused to the arraignment, which takes place before a magistrate or judge who advises the accused of the charges against him. Generally, a Bond or Condition of Release is established at this appearance.

The public defender will handle all the essential documents and hearings for the accused. The accused should read and familiarize himself with each and every document pertaining to the case and try to understand every charge against him.

It is important to note that the public defender is representing the accused only. The attorney cannot share information about the case with anyone other than the accused unless he has permission from the accused; and, even then, there may be limits on what an attorney is likely to share with a spouse or family member.

A public defender is required to provide adequate time to prepare each case; however, he is often assisted by a paralegal, who is assigned to meet with the defendant and his family when there are documents to be signed and to explain pleadings, police reports, or other information pertinent to the case.

Plea-Agreements

Do not be surprised if your attorney suggests a plea-agreement; most criminal cases result in a plea-agreement. This course of action is not a reflection of a lazy attorney; rather, it is the recommendation when it is the best possible option. In fact, under the Federal Sentencing Guidelines, a sentence is generally reduced if the accused accepts a plea-agreement and pleads guilty. However, an attorney is required to present the plea-agreement offered by the prosecution whether he recommends the plea or not.

At all times, the defendant has the option to refuse the attorney's advice and go to trial; yet, he must listen carefully to his counsel. Attorneys understand the legal system and know the pros and cons of a particular case going to trial. Give a public defender the benefit of the doubt. He is there to help and will usually perform more than adequate legal representation.

Once the trial is completed with a guilty verdict and the defendant is sentenced, the public defender's job is over. There is generally no further contact between the defendant and the public defender. Public defenders are not social workers; they are not paid to handle post-trial situations, such as emergency furloughs or parole.

Bond and Bail

Bail is defined as money or credit deposited with the court to get an arrested person temporarily released on the assurance that he will appear in court at an appointed date. A bond is a certificate, an evidence of a debt, which secures bail. It allows release from jail for the accused within the jurisdiction of the court.

In all cases, court fees and fines will be assessed and need to be paid according to the guidelines established by the court. All court fees will be over and above any money paid to make bail. Court fees may be as low as fifty dollars, but consult with your attorney so that you are prepared to pay these fees at the appropriate time.

~Five Options to Make Bond
Remember: Consult your attorney.
1. Bondsman or Surety Company
2. Percentage to the Courts
3. Property or Collateral Bond
4. Cash
5. Release-on-Recognizance (ROR)

1. Bondsman or Surety Company
If the court allows and establishes the cash amount of bail, the accused will be released from jail following payment to a registered bondsman or surety company. A surety company is defined as one who becomes liable for another person's debts or defaults on obligations. A bondsman's fee is usually ten percent of the bond and payment is due upon agreement of the bond. The bondsman's ten percent will not be returned to you after the court appearance of the accused. The ten percent is the fee you pay them for the risk they take in paying your total bond owed to the court.

A co-signer is usually required to obtain a bond. A co-signer must prove employment with one company for a time period of two to three years, own property, or both. The co-signer must sign a Promissory Note that is a legal and binding contract, making him liable for the full amount of the bond if the accused does not show up in court.

To make bond in another state, fifteen percent of the bail is assessed in order to cover the additional cost of a transfer fee.

After paying the fifteen percent, the bondsman will contact a bondsman or surety company in the appropriate state to arrange the bond. The fees that are charged by each surety company are usually monitored and set by each state. An out of state bondsman is usually picked on the merits of convenience, professionalism, and service. These are generalities and not every state allows for this transfer. Again, check with an attorney before making any decisions.

2. Percentage to the Courts

The judge determines the percentage of the bond, just as he sets the bond amount. Ten percent of the bond is most common, but twenty percent or higher is allowable. The judge has complete control over this matter. You may need to use a bondsman to help you pay the ten percent to the court.

3. Property Bond or Collateral

When agreeing to a collateral bond, property may be used as collateral—a guarantee against the bond. But, this method can be very time consuming. Property appraisals are usually required and there is considerable documentation needed to give temporary ownership of the property to the court. The advantage of this method is that upon court appearance and settlement of case, the property reverts back to the owner. The bond does not cost anything, but the accused may have to remain in jail for several days while the appropriate documentation is completed. If the equity of the property doesn't cover the amount of the bond, you may still have to use your property as collateral for a bondsman. Remember, whenever you use the services of a bondsman, be prepared to pay ten percent of the amount of the bond to him.

4. Cash

Cash payment is the most efficient method of making bond. When the accused shows up for trial and the case is settled, the cash will be returned.

5. Release-On-Recognizance (ROR)

ROR is offered if the accused's crime warrants relaxed treatment by the court and his reputation indicates that he is not a flight risk.

God gave burdens, also shoulders.

—Yiddish Proverb

3

After the Arrest

Facing Your Community

It is not easy discussing a loved one's arrest among family or friends. This is already a difficult time, and to make matters worse the local news media may print incorrect details of the story, causing more complications for your family. Although people may realize they should not believe everything reported in the local media, once something is in print or on TV it is usually perceived as the truth. You may want to ignore newscasts and newspaper articles for a while, since news reports often include more than the hard facts. Even minor errors or misrepresentations of your loved one's case can make everyone in the family feel angry and defeated. Therefore, as the pressure around your family mounts, it is essential to stay in touch with each other. You must share your feelings. You are struggling for emotional survival.

Friends and Neighbors

Your friends and neighbors will probably not know how to respond to the indictment and arrest of someone close to them. They may hear about it on television or read about it in the newspaper, and they may be uncertain about asking you questions. You will soon have to decide who, among your neighbors and community, are genuinely concerned with your plight and want to help.

Do not assume that people who ask questions are being inconsiderate or nosy. They may just want to receive the facts from a believable source. Be brief, but honest. You do not have to share details, but help your close friends—people you trust and can lean on—to understand your predicament. However, you may want to tell friends that your attorney has discouraged discussion of the case with friends. **Warning:** People that you share material information with may be called as witnesses. Moreover, if you tesify in court, but your story differs from the story you shared with friends/witnesses, they may be called to the stand to account for differences in the story you shared with them, which would impeach your testimony.

Following the arrest of a loved one you will discover rather quickly who your friends are. If people cannot be counted upon to help you and your family get through this challenging time in your life, let them go.

Prior to my husband's arrest, I had been the Cub Scout leader of my oldest son's troop. I devoted a great deal of time and enthusiasm to the troop, which, in turn, was reflected in the number of merit badges that the boys earned. However, shortly after my husband's indictment, several parents voiced concerns to the headmistress. They felt that I was no longer an ideal role model for the Cub Scout organization and demanded my resignation. Fortunately, the headmistress recognized my devotion and benefit to the organization and overturned the parents' decision. From this experience, I fully realized the importance of a true friend. When you find unique people who continue to believe in you, take time to thank them and rejoice the value of their friendship.

Helping Children and Teenagers Cope

If you have children in school, inform their teachers of your legal situation so that they may clarify and suppress harmful school rumors. A loving teacher or supportive principal/counselor can be a godsend for your child during this time. By giving your children's teachers adequate information, you enable them to handle problems with tact and compassion. Your children will need their support.

Younger children do not need to know all of the details of a family member's arrest and impending trial. They do need to know that someone they love is having legal problems. If they ask further questions about legal difficulties, do not lie. Give them accurate information, but not so much that they worry and fret about the upcoming trial. It may be impossible, however, to keep even young children from hearing details of a parent's charges from friends and schoolmates whose parents may discuss the case. Therefore, it is better that they hear the truth from you rather than hear the story through gossip.

You may want to keep headlines and newspaper stories about the case from children's eyes. Shield your young children from unkind remarks. Hearing that someone they love is a "criminal" can be destructive to young children. Realize that young children are vulnerable, and that the incarceration of a loved one, especially of a father, is going to be emotionally traumatic for them. Keep young children guarded from the emotional and legal struggles of this period.

Just as children may blame themselves for a divorce in the family, they may also find a reason to place the blame on themselves for a legal problem. For example, if a child had been asking for a new bike, and then his father was caught stealing money, they may associate the two events and feel responsible for the outcome. Unfortunately, children often find ways to blame themselves for terrible things that adults do. It is very important to explain that they are not responsible.

WARNING: For Parents of Teenagers

For teenagers, the shock of arrest and subsequent negative publicity about their family can be overwhelming. Not only are teenagers extremely peer conscious; but, unlike young children, teenagers cannot be kept from newspapers and television coverage.

Parents of teenagers should expect huge emotional and behavioral swings. One moment teenagers may appear calm and understanding, and in the next moment they may be announcing that they are leaving home. They may lock themselves in their room for hours. Some may disregard all family rules and engage in disruptive behavior within the family and at school. They may announce hatred and disgust for the person responsible for the familial upheaval. Teenagers may easily turn to alcohol and drugs and be drawn to peer groups with destructive habits. Be alert and pay attention to your teenagers' behavior and habits.

The Warning Signs

- Spending excessive time alone
- Altered sleeping habits
- Loss of appetite
- Leaving the house at unusual hours
- Lying
- Drastic change in style of wardrobe
- Unexplained extra money or material items; i.e., cell

phone, expensive clothing and shoes, jewelry

School counselors and teachers may be a source of support during this time. Therefore, don't be shy to ask for help. Communicate with guidance counselors, teachers, and other parents about your teenager. Ask the school counselor and your teen's teachers to observe your teen and report unusual or abusive behavior. Do not be so caught up in your own emotions and frustrations that you forget the needs of your teenager. Be available to your teenager and communicate your love and support. Give your teenager love and understanding through this difficult period. You are investing in your family's future and they are only young once.

For Better and For Worse: Holding Together a Marriage

Few, if any couples, are prepared for the emotional upheaval that serious legal problems bring to a marriage. If a marriage is to survive, open and honest discussion is imperative. A husband who has been arrested must understand that his wife has become the innocent victim of his actions. Subsequently, she is probably going to be very angry, finding several personal and professional choices have become limited. This was especially true in my life. I grew up in an all-American town with a loving family, who encouraged my path of successful endeavors: first female Student Council President in my high school, Cheerleading Captain, Who's Who in American High Schools and Colleges, Phi Beta Kappa, University Homecoming Queen, Outstanding Delta Zeta in the United States, Miss Michigan contestant, flight attendant, and real estate broker. To add to that, I had a loving marriage and four precious sons. I felt respected by the public and was confident in myself. However, as soon as my husband was arrested, none of my accomplishments were taken into consideration anymore. I became the wife of the accused, and for all practical purposes, I was treated as such. My identity was judged by my spouse's reputation.

It is very difficult to remain calm and composed throughout the period between the indictment and the actual trial. Anger and frustration are likely to erupt between marriage partners. The spouse of the accused must be allowed to acknowledge her anger to herself and to her husband and should, furthermore, be encouraged to recognize her anger and feelings of helplessness. If there is to be future reconciliation and family harmony, she must be given the opportunity to tell her spouse just how disappointed she is with his actions.

Suggestions for the Accused

Following an arrest and release on bail, the accused should expect to find those closest to him angry and confused by his alleged actions. He must recognize that he has brought his loved ones pain, suffering, embarrassment, and lifestyle changes. If the accused wants his spouse and family to stand beside him during the trial and wait for him during the months or years of a possible prison sentence, then it is up to him to begin the healing process by accepting responsibility for his charges. He must address the difficulties at hand. He must not fight back, but listen. And, furthermore, he should not only try to comfort his wife, seeking her support and love throughout this time; but, he should also apologize for the emotional and social storm his arrest has brought upon his family.

For the Accused:

If you blame others for your legal problems or refuse to acknowledge the harm you have done to your family, you may lose understanding and support from your family.

Pre-Trial

The period before the trial or plea-bargaining is a time of uncertainty for a married couple and their family. Until the case has been tried, the future is completely unknown. Any constructive work or activities not related to the trial will probably be put on hold, and an attorney suddenly becomes the main touchstone.

If the accused owns a company, his business may falter. Investors and clients generally do not want to deal with someone who may go to prison. If the accused is employed, he may find his employer anxious to let him go. The employer may wish to replace him with someone who will not bring negative publicity to the business. The accused, although not yet convicted, will be treated as if he has been found guilty of whatever crime he stands accused. The accused will be very dependent on the support of friends and family while awaiting trial.

Meetings with the attorney will take precedence over all other matters. There will be numerous private conversations between the accused and his attorney; however, these conversations should be shared later with the family.

Plea-bargain vs. Trial

If an attorney recommends a plea-bargain, make sure he explains all factors and consequences of the statements in the plea-bargain. Opting for a plea-bargain usually indicates that the attorney believes the accused is not going to win. Hence, a plea-bargain is an attempt to lessen the punishment/prison time issued by the court.

If an attorney decides that the case should go to trial, educate yourself about the law pertaining to your loved one's case. Understand that your present and past life is going to be an open book in the court and in the newspapers. Standing beside the accused is bound to test your courage and love.

Remember, whether your loved one chooses to plea-bargain or go to trial, you should be involved in the decision-making process. Although your loved one will serve the sentence in prison, choosing to remain married to him leaves you to do your own "time" as you wait for him.

Preparing for Incarceration and Separation
If your spouse is going to spend time in prison, there are several matters to address that will help make life easier during the period of incarceration.

"To Do" List For the Accused
1. Spend the majority of your time with loved ones.

2. Spend time with your immediate family. This group will probably provide your greatest support. Give to them now, as you will need to receive from them later.

3. Organize your finances. Introduce your spouse to your banker, creditors, and IRS agents to explain the current and future status of your finances.

4. If belongings need to be placed in a storage unit, box and label items. Evaluate your finances to ensure that all storage payments can be made. If a payment is missed, the storage company will sell your items. You may want to arrange free storage with a friend or family member.

5. Get a complete physical exam in order to address health conditions prior to incarceration. Establishing required prescriptions will allow you to receive them during incarceration. Check your cholesterol, prostate, colon, and have an EKG performed. Once you are incarcerated,

it will be difficult to obtain a specialist.

6. If you require medication, have a full prescription prepared for your entrance into incarceration.

7. Prepare a copy of your medical records so they may be mailed to you if needed.

8. Have your eyes examined. Make a copy of your prescription for future use. If you require glasses or contacts, purchase them prior to incarceration, as they are very expensive to order through the prison system. Suggestion: purchase two.

9. Complete all dental work. Request a copy of your X-Rays and keep them with your health records. If you are unable to complete dental work, obtain a written diagnosis from your dentist for the prison dental facility.

10. If you will be allowed to wear civilian clothes in the institution you will be placed in, determine which items you want to be mailed to you. Choose clothing relative to the climate of the prison's location, taking all seasons into consideration, and select clothing on the basis of comfort and durability. Importantly, adhere to all clothing policies of the institution. Remember, you will be limited to a small number of undergarments and socks, so make your choices wisely and write your choices on paper for the family member who will be shopping for you.

11. Choose a comfortable pair of shoes for your time of incarceration. Military-styled boots are often the issued footwear for prisoners. But, these boots tend to be heavy,

hot, and impractical for recreational use. Since time is devoted to recreation on a daily basis, choose footwear according to comfort and prison policy.

12. Update your driver's license. Although you will not be allowed to hold a DL in prison, you will need one in order to go to a halfway house after your sentence is completed. In addition, if you are selected to be a driver for your prison, you will need to have your current DL mailed to you.

13. Purchase an inexpensive, water resistant watch. Most penal institutions will not allow an inmate to possess a watch valued over $100.00.

14. Change the mailing address of your magazine subscriptions to the prison's address.

15. Sign a Power-of-Attorney document for your spouse or family member, which will allow that person to sign legal documents on your behalf while you are in prison.

The Defendant's Day in Court

The defendant's first time in court will be for the arraignment, the second time for the plea-agreement or the trial, and the last time will be for the sentencing. I recommend that most family members try to attend each of the three court hearings to show support on behalf of the defendant. Do not take anyone with you who will require personal attention or distract you from the court proceedings. Every word that is said in court will be important for you to hear and analyze.

Remain in control of your emotions while in the courtroom. You will not be allowed to mutter under your breath, make deep sighs, cry out loud, or disturb the judge and jury. You will be asked to leave the courtroom if your behavior becomes distracting. Your attitude and demeanor in the courtroom may positively or negatively influence the judge and jury. Obviously, you want your appearance to be viewed as positively as possible. Therefore, try to "blend into the woodwork," becoming a stable force for your loved one.

Be prepared for the media. Generally it is best to not make any statements to the press. Refer any questions to your attorney if you anticipate media coverage and always try to be in control of your emotions publicly. Be careful to never discuss your case outside the courtroom, in hallways, or in bathrooms where your remarks could be picked up by a reporter. It is best for your attorney to handle the press and all public statements. Unless you are required to testify, your personal comments are best shared only with family and close friends in a private setting.

Dressing for Court

I recommend that women wear a conservative suit or dress. Your appearance should be one of respect towards the judge and his court. Do not wear anything sexy or provocative. Your attire should not suggest in any way that you are trying to influence the judge and jury in an inappropriate manner. Avoid wearing short skirts, low cut blouses, or tight tank tops. Wear under garments. If you feel you do not have clothes that would be appropriate for court and you are living on a small budget, look for conservative clothing in a thrift store.

Men should wear a suit or a sport coat, pressed trousers, and a tie. Blue jeans and sneakers, as well as baseball caps and cowboy hats, are inappropriate for a court appearance.

Be well groomed for court. Wash and style your hair, wear cosmetics in a conservative fashion, and generally look your best. Imagining you are going to a Sunday worship service or business meeting should help you identify clothing that would be appropriate for the courtroom.

If children will be in court with you, these clothing guidelines apply to them as well. Most children will not understand the court proceedings and find them boring and confusing. However, they must remain quiet; therefore, you may want to pack small bags for them, which could have snacks, coloring books, markers, or illustrated books to keep them occupied. Food is not allowed in the courtroom, but during breaks they may eat their snacks in the hallway.

What Really Matters

The weeks spent waiting for the trial can be used to strengthen a marriage and family. Focus on what is most important. If a prison sentence seems imminent, make the remaining days before the trial special. Spend time with the children doing activities they enjoy. The simplest events can be the most important—fishing with a son, reading to a daughter, or watching a family movie. Be sure to find time to play and spend plenty of time laughing. Make sure the one who is going to prison knows how much he is loved and needed in the family. Make this time, although stressful and full of doubts and unanswered questions, a time to remember and cherish. Try to take plenty of photographs, which will lend to creating positive memories.

There is no failure except in no longer trying.
—Elbert Hubbard

4

Options

After the accused has been released on bail, and you are awaiting his trial, you will be faced with several options:
1. Run
2. Escape through drugs/alcohol
3. Suicide
4. Divorce
5. Face the problem

Option 1: Running from the Law
Knowing your loved one will be spending a significant amount of time in prison may cause you and him to consider an escape attempt. Before deciding on this option, be sure you have weighed all the consequences. Police departments across the country, and even throughout the world, are linked by computers. Running with the accused will necessitate changing your identity to avoid being caught. You will never be able to contact

anyone you have known, and you will criminally charged. You will enter a life that has no past, and you will never be able to comfortably visit your previous home or community.

Running from the law can be very expensive. Forged identification cards, passports, and credit cards are documents that will be difficult to obtain, even illegally, and you will need to pay cash for each of them. Without a past employment record, finding employment will be difficult. You will be dealing with the underworld, and the compromises you may be forced to make will be numerous. If children are involved, their lives will become very complicated and confusing. Running from the law will cause you to be suspicious of strangers and afraid of every policeman. Do not run! Stay and work through your problems.

Option 2: Escapism Through Drugs and Alcohol

Narcotics and alcohol provide escape from reality; unfortunately, the escape is only temporary and it may leave you with the added problems of drug addiction and alcoholism.

Drug abuse will threaten your loved one's bail status. Assuming he has made bail, he will be given a Urine Analysis (UA) that tests for possible drug use even if his offense is not drug related. A "dirty U.A." (see glossary) can result in immediate incarceration and revocation of bond. Do not let your loved one or yourself turn to drugs. Drug charges bring about very serious penalties. You are already dealing with one offense; don't add drug related charges to your case.

If your case involved drug charges, encourage your loved one to voluntarily enter a drug rehabilitation center. This will help him to become drug free and avoid further charges during pre-trial drug testing. Voluntary participation in a drug rehabilitation program shows the court that the accused is willing to take the initiative to rid himself of a drug addiction.

When drugs are involved in the arrest, attendance at

Narcotics Anonymous (NA) or Alcoholics Anonymous (AA) is often required during the prison term. Upon release from prison, those with drug sentences usually continue drug testing on a weekly basis throughout the duration of parole.

Like narcotics, alcohol may seem to lessen the burden for a few hours; but, ultimately, drinking will inflate the problems. Effective communication between family members is greatly diminished when someone is drinking. Alcohol abuse can splinter what is left of a family and leave the accused alone at trial. Do not allow anyone in the family to engage in drug or alcohol abuse before trial. Everyone needs to be clear and focused. Do not give the prosecutor an edge even before you enter the courtroom. Be smart: stay sober.

Option 3: Suicide

Suicide may seem like an appealing option to the one facing incarceration, but suicide does not make the problems disappear for those who are left behind. For a spouse and family, the suicide of an accused is the beginning of a new nightmare. The bills do not go away and the legal problems do not vanish.

If suicide is being considered by any member of the family, please contact a suicide hotline immediately. Moreover, most communities offer free counseling to those who can't afford the cost of mental health therapy.

Option 4: Divorce

Legal troubles will probably unleash emotional exchanges between spouses. As the wife of the accused, you may ask yourself: What do I want from this marriage? What are my options? Can I remain loyal to this partner who is the source of all this pain?

Before divorcing a spouse facing a prison sentence, carefully weigh your emotional balance. Is your dissatisfaction and anger created by the legal problems brought upon your family by your spouse? Will these feelings of anger and disappointment lessen as time passes? Or, is your dissatisfaction actually based on years of destructive behavior?

If you have been physically or emotionally battered, you have sound reason to leave the marriage. Now may be a very good time to end an abusive relationship and move forward with your life.

Talk with friends. Seek out a counselor. Join a support group. Ask for the advice of a pastor, priest, rabbi, or someone else's opinion that you value. Clergy are still the most available caregivers in America.

Let's face it, there are many advantages to divorcing a spouse who is going to prison. It may become easier to deal with the IRS and other governmental agencies as a divorced person. It may be a relief to face your friends and community having disconnected from someone going to prison. You are at least giving yourself a fresh start. If you cannot forgive your spouse for his illegal indiscretions and now choose divorce, spare yourself the guilt trip.

Option 5: Face the Problem

Facing the problem at hand is never easy. Suddenly, there is much in your daily life that is unknown and unsettled. And dealing with attorneys, prosecutors, judges, juries, and jails overwhelms most people. Therefore, the best path through the legal maze is taken one day at a time, and on some days, one hour at a time. Facing this challenge as a couple or as a family will give you real comfort and strength. Ask for help from friends and family and engage in honest communication in order to give yourself a sense of security and balance throughout this difficult crisis. I know; I did it. Others have survived and you can too. Start by getting your home life under control. Put aside all trivial activities and worries and concentrate on your case. Knowledge and preparation are the best skills you can develop for survival.

Accept the challenges, so that you may feel the exhilaration of victory.

—General George S. Patton

5

Understanding the Law

Your Attorney

Your attorney is going to be your number one source of information and legal advice. Listen to your attorney and ask questions. Discuss options. Most importantly, take your attorney's advice and follow his directions inside and outside of the courtroom.

PSI: Pre-Sentence Investigation

The PSI, or Pre-Sentence Investigation, is probably the most important document that will be filed about your loved one and his crime. The PSI is the one document that is referred to and influences decisions made about the accused *before* sentencing, *during* incarceration, and *after* incarceration.

The PSI is written by Pre-Trial Services, a division of the probation department, and delineates the character of the accused and his cause for committing the crime. Unfortunately, the PSI is often given to the accused only ten minutes before sentencing. Obviously, this does not give him an appropriate amount of time to accurately evaluate the document. I suggest that the PSI be read carefully. If there is inaccurate information in the PSI, or information that may discredit the accused, try to have the report changed before sentencing. If the PSI is not accurate, check immediately with your attorney about delaying the sentencing until the PSI is changed. It is very important that the information about the accused be as accurate as possible. At a later date, this information may be used to determine whether he is a candidate for early halfway house release, or if he could be moved to a less restricted level of the prison in accordance with "non-violent" behavior. If there is any wording in the PSI about the accused being a drug user, this will haunt the accused for years to come. It is likely that while incarcerated the accused will be required to attend drug-related seminars, 12-step programs, or similar treatment sessions. And, there will be frequent drug testing. The additional problem of having "drug user" listed on the PSI is that when he finally gets released from prison, he may still be required to attend drug rehabilitation programs. This attendance at the meetings may be required for months or even years after returning to society as a "free man," but still on parole. Urine testing at a halfway house will also be more frequent for an inmate that has drug usage mentioned on the PSI.

If firearms are mentioned in the PSI, it will be very difficult to shed a positive light on the case, and the accused will probably be directed to an institution that maintains a higher level of security.

Again, the PSI is a highly important document. Even if the inmate has a flawless prison record, the PSI will be utilized at the time of the inmate's release to determine his future status. In addition, the PSI may help the judge determine whether the accused is a candidate for self-surrender, or, if he can't be trust-ed, face immediate arrest, and be sent from a detention center to prison. "Diesel-bus therapy" is the term used by inmates that refers to the method of moving inmates from detention centers to prisons or transferring them from one prison to another. Usually the inmates are chained and shackled while being moved from one county jail to the next. This process can last a few days, several months, or even a year before the prisoners reach their final destination.

"Diesel-bus therapy" is not a pleasant situation to be in. Typically, the inmates are awakened in the county jail at dawn and ushered quickly onto the bus, then driven to other institutions to pick up new inmates. However, often the bus has to wait hours for the final processing of new inmates before the trip continues. The bus makes frequent stops, and it is quite typical for this pro-cedure to continue until late into the evening. Often, the inmates spend the night in another county jail, and upon arrival at the jail, they are usually strip searched. It is often difficult to make phone calls while on "diesel-bus therapy" and family members have been known to go for weeks without hearing from their loved one. Cigarettes and essentials, such as toothbrushes, toothpaste, and combs, are difficult to obtain, as there is no commissary where these items can be purchased. An inmate may make the entire trip without some of these basic items.

Sentencing Fines

Sentencing fines and IRS issues are highly important. If part of the inmate's sentence includes paying back a fine, under-stand the payment schedule. The fine may be expected to be par-tially paid back from money earned while in prison. Many jobs in prison pay as little as $.10 per hour, or may go as high as $1.15 per hour, with overtime pay possible for inmates employed by UNICOR. However, the fine may make life very difficult for him

in prison, as he may not have enough money to purchase necessary items from the commissary as needed. He may be forced to
ask for outside financial assistance from family and friends.

Fines that are required to be paid when the inmate is
released from prison are a very difficult undertaking. Securing a
job may pose a problem, and once he acquires a job, he may barely earn enough money to cover his living requirements. The lin-
gering debt may hinder employment from the onset, since a
potential employer may run a credit report and discover this obli-
gation, creating reluctance to hire. Legally, the debt shouldn't
affect whether he is hired or not. Yet, my credit report *has* denied
me access to jobs; therefore, don't fool yourself into thinking
that it might not affect you as well. Remember, I was the wife of
the prisoner, not the prisoner. I recommend an arrangement in
which an additional six months or one year of time is added to
the sentence to reduce a high fine. It is important to consider the
impact that the fine will have on the inmate's life, as it could take
several years to repay. Some former inmates are never able to
fully repay their fines and struggle with that debt the rest of their
lives.

The IRS

In the plea-agreement my husband signed, he didn't realize the importance of settling the civil IRS issues in the plea-
agreement. Over the sixteen years that have passed since my husband's arrest, I've met with thirty-one IRS agents and countless
State Revenue Officers, and I have been forced to represent
myself (Pro Se). The largest problem presented to me was an IRS
debt of over $3.5 million dollars. As I met with each of the
agents over the years, I consistently explained my financial situation and presented all the documents they required, which
involved extensive preparation on my part. Of course, I can't
even begin to describe the worry, fear, and dread I experienced

before each meeting.

A few months after my husband left for prison, the IRS wanted me to sign a document stating that we owed the IRS a certain amount of money. Since I felt that we didn't owe that amount of money, I refused to sign the document, as I would have been responsible to pay that amount. Because I refused to sign the document, I had to fight the IRS in court.

During the time I was battling the IRS in court, I still had an infant on oxygen who needed twenty-four hour attention. So, we both went to court. I stood before the IRS and a judge scared to death. My husband was already in prison, I had four little boys that needed me for survival, and I was warned that if I perjured myself I could be thrown in jail. Moreover, an IRS agent told me that if I went to jail he would make sure my four boys were put in foster homes in each of the four corners of the United States and I would never see them again. Needless to say, I was terrified.

The final outcome of the case, one which resulted in hundreds of thousands of dollars in legal fees paid to the IRS attorneys by the U.S. taxpayers, was my signature on a document stating that I "agreed to disagree" about the amount of debt that the IRS said I owed. Essentially, nothing was accomplished by the IRS forcing me into court proceedings.

Until 1988, IRS liens could be renewed every seven years. Now liens remain on a person's record for a minimum of ten years, even though one of the agents I had met with told me that the lien the IRS held against me could be renewed every ten years for the rest of my life. I can't tell you how frustrating it is to have no money, be told that any income I made over $30,000.00 would be garnished by the IRS, and have no ability to ever repay the total debt. The threat of garnished wages condemned me to living near the poverty level as I raised my four boys.

However, this particular story has a good ending. The laws have changed. I was first told about an "Offer-in-

Compromise" that is an agreement between the IRS and the indebted party, which enables the indebted party to pay an amount that they can afford to pay in order to make good on the debt. Obviously, I would never have been able to repay $3.5 million dollars, and even a small percentage of that would have been impossible for me to repay.

I was then notified about "Innocent Spouse Relief" Form 8857, a law drawn up in 1998. Due to that law, I finally received relief. I also found out that several former IRS agents had lied to me in the past. The boys could not have been taken from me and put in foster homes across the country. I could have made over $30,000.00 each year and my earnings would not have been garnished. IRS liens may be released from a person's record after ten years; however, some IRS agents had told me that they could renew the liens every ten years until I died and then they would attach the liens to my boys' records. This is definitely not true; the liens cannot be attached to another person.

I thought my husband went to prison to pay his debt to society; yet, we, the spouse and children of the prisoner, were forced to pay his debt for fifteen years. IRS liens and fines are not to be taken lightly. They haunted me for years after my husband's incarceration. The time to do something about them is before a plea-agreement is negotiated. Try to eliminate any fines and/or IRS liens from your record.

Letters to the Prosecutor and Judge

Prior to sentencing it may be permissible for a wife or family members to write a letter to the prosecuting attorney and the judge. In this letter, wives and family members have the opportunity to give the prosecutor and the judge some facts about the accused's family and personal history. A letter informs the judge and prosecutor that there are people who care about the welfare of the defendant. Remember, the judge and prosecuting attorney are busy professionals; therefore, keep the letters brief and to the point. Type or neatly handwrite letters to the judge and prosecutor. Stick to the facts and never make false statements or write about irrelevant issues. Be sincere. Essentially, explain your family situation and declare your support for your spouse. Your letters will become part of your spouse's permanent file. It is possible that in the future your letters could prove beneficial to your spouse regarding community custody, social furloughs, community work projects, and length of stay at a halfway house. According to statistics, a convicted felon has a better chance of adjusting to the real world after prison if he has a family that loves and cares about him during incarceration.

You may also write to the judge and prosecuting attorney after your husband has entered prison. I wrote letters twice a year—near the anniversary of my husband's prison sentence, and at Christmas time. Although your theme may be the same, try to use different words and phrases. Keep copies of your letters at home so that you can refer to them each year. Send your letters to the judge or prosecuting attorney by the U.S. Postal Service Certified Mail, Return Receipt Requested. This way you will know that the proper office has received your letter. The purpose of this type of letter writing could also prove beneficial many years later for relocation purposes, early release from parole, or probation.

Letters may also prove especially helpful if there is recidivism (a return to prison) involved. For instance, the court system is generally less tolerant of a repeat offender; however, letters of support from the offender's family may encourage some leniency.

Families Against Mandatory Minimums
The non-profit national organization, Families Against Mandatory Minimums (FAMM), was founded in 1991. There are

currently over 25,000 members, including prisoners and their families, concerned citizens, attorneys, judges, and criminal justice experts. The goal of FAMM is to restore the rights of the judges to determine each individual sentence. When a judge is forced to use mandatory sentencing laws, it prevents him from using his judgment and does not allow any flexibility in sentencing.

FAMM's national headquarters resides in Washington, D.C., but there are local chapters in many states. FAMM's objective is to educate the public about unfair mandatory sentencing, lobby state and federal lawmakers to end mandatory sentencing requirements, and mobilize concerned citizens into a powerful sentencing reform movement. To join FAMM or get more information about this organization, contact them at 1-202-822-6700 or visit their website at www.famm.org

Survival Skills *for the* Family

stage

II

The mighty oak tree was once a little nut that held its ground.
—Modern Proverb

6

Home Alone

For Wives: Life Alone

The day my husband left for prison, I was very angry with him for actions that caused him to be taken from our family. There were so many loose ends in my life, including unpaid bills, insurance problems, and unpleasant calls from bankers, lawyers, and IRS representatives. Plus, I was left with four children that depended completely on me. My anger replaced my desire to have my husband at home with me, but that feeling was short lived. The reality of raising my sons, dealing with our financial affairs, and facing life at home alone quickly overwhelmed me.

After your husband leaves for prison, you are going to feel very alone and experience self-pity. Accept those feelings. Your husband has not only created problems for you, he has left you to struggle through them alone. It will be natural to feel confused and depressed. You will experience feelings of loss and shock similar to what a widow feels upon the death of a husband. But there are two very important differences: your husband may return to you in the future, and his absence is surrounded by negative social stigmas. Unlike a widow, it seems as if no one feels sorry for the wife of a convicted criminal, who is left to fend for herself. In many instances, the wife is treated as if she were as guilty as the prisoner. This happened time after time to me, and this constant feeling of being looked down upon can frustrate the strongest person. Ultimately, you must learn to survive the separation, heal emotional wounds, and accept and understand your life so that you may go into the future with a positive spirit.

Spend time with those friends who truly care about your well being. Allow friends and family to worry about you, to call frequently, and check up on you. Accept their concern. If you have a rabbi, priest, minister, or social worker with whom you can talk openly about your feelings, schedule time for this. If you can arrange time with a counselor or psychologist, see one on a regular basis. Do not isolate yourself during this time; you are facing a tremendous loss.

Stages of Emotional Recovery

1. Shock and denial of the loss

The body reacts with numbness, which is our protection against intense pain. The mind pretends the loss has not happened; therefore, we refuse to acknowledge what has occurred.

2. Depression, fear, and anger

This stage of recovery can seem to go on for months or years. As difficult as these emotions can be, they are a natural and necessary part of healing after loss.

3. Acceptance and understanding

Acceptance results in the ability to move forward in life. We look back and see that we have survived a difficult, painful period in our lives. We are strengthened by our survival. We see that life is possible without the loved one who has been taken away. We accept our new lives.

Each of these stages of recovery are necessary and can overlap with one another. Trust the body and mind's natural healing process. Talk with others who have endured grief and loss. Understand that there will be an end to the pain and confusion.

Focus on Life: Focus on You

Keep a positive outlook and believe that things are going to get better and that you will succeed. Understand that the pain you are feeling is actually the way the body and the mind undergo the healing process. Give yourself reasons to get up in the morning. If you haven't done something fun for yourself or with your children in a while, plan fun, low cost activities. Give your children and yourself events to look forward to, such as a picnic lunch at the park, a swim at the city pool, a visit with grandparents, or a game of cards.

There may be days that you will want to lie in bed and cry all day; that is okay. But after a long cry, get out of bed. You will find the urge to cry lessens when you become more active. Yet, the grieving and healing process does not progress in a smooth, uphill manner. Some days you will feel better; other days you will feel as if you have slid backwards into the old depression. You probably have. But that's part of the healing process. You may be unable to concentrate on work, lose your appetite, develop insomnia, and feel tired and helpless. These are all natural reactions to the loss of a loved one.

Responding to Difficult Questions

One of the most difficult questions I had to field was, "Where is your husband?" Although I thought everyone in the world knew that he was locked up in prison, some people were simply inquiring why he wasn't escorting me to a particular function. In order to save myself from having to explain the unpleasant details of my husband's whereabouts, I would simply respond, "We're separated." Since separation is common in today's society, that response generally halted any further interrogation in a social setting.

Although I was becoming accustomed to my "prisoner's wife" stigma, the immediate betrayal on the part of my insurance agent came as a shock. Not only were my husband and I clients of our insurance agent for over twelve years, but we offered our home in Jamaica to him for his honeymoon and, over many years, enjoyed several cherished dinners and events together. Yet, shortly after my husband entered prison, I received a notice in the mail that our insurance was canceled. I placed several phone calls to our insurance agency, but our "dear" friend and insurance agent never returned my calls, nor have I heard from him since.

Ultimately, I was left to acquire insurance with a new carrier; however, explaining my husband's absence to insurance agents became a task that required strategy. Like most experiences, I learned my strategy through trial and error. When I began placing calls to insurance agents, the conversations took the following direction:

INSURANCE COMPANY A

Agent: "Are you married?"
Me: "Yes."
Agent: "Then both of you will be driving the car?"
Me: "No. Actually, he won't be driving."
Agent: "Why not?"

Me: "Well, my husband is serving a fifteen year sentence in prison, so I know he won't be driving for many years."
Agent: "Oh. I'm sorry, but we won't be able to insure you."

INSURANCE COMPANY B

Agent: "Why was your insurance canceled?"
Me: "Well, due to a slight problem, the company will no longer insure us."
Agent: "What problem is that?"
Me: "My husband is in prison."
Agent: "Oh. In that case, we can insure you, but I will have to double the rate I just quoted you."
Me: "Double the quote? Why?"
Agent: "He is in prison, and when he gets out he may want to steal your car."

INSURANCE COMPANY C (My New Strategy)

Agent: "Why was your insurance canceled?"
Me: "Unfortunately, I had a slight problem with my husband."
Agent: "What was the problem?"
Me: "I became separated from my husband and the bills just kind of got misplaced, and, well, you can imagine the rest."
Agent: "I understand. We can insure you, but the rate will increase somewhat from the amount you were previously paying."

By claiming delinquent payments, but avoiding the issue of prison, I was simply considered a financial risk and was offered insurance at a higher rate. But, I was not turned down. So, I learned to phrase my answers creatively in order to avoid the severe judgement of having a husband in prison.

Another difficult question that arose was, "What does your husband do for a living?" I didn't want to lie, but I also didn't want to divulge his prison status. So, I would cleverly respond, "My husband works for the government." In essence, he did work for the government; in fact, he earned eleven cents per hour.

I am not suggesting that you lie or deceive people, but there are situations which require creative thinking when your husband's socially unacceptable status is the topic at hand. Therefore, while you are burdened by the "prisoner's wife" stigma, utilize my responses to craft safe answers to difficult questions.

Dare to be what you ought to be; dare to be what you dream to be; dare to be the finest you can be. The more you dare, the surer you will be of gaining just what you dare!

—Norman Vincent Peale

7

The Home Front

Once your spouse is in prison, it is time to fortify your family home and daily routine. It is imperative to focus on your goals, the children, your job, and a positive outlook toward life. Circle the family wagons and regroup. You are stepping into a new frontier and you are the family's wagon master.

Single Parenting

For all practical purposes, once your spouse is incarcerated, you have become a single parent. Your husband may continue to discuss the children with you over the phone or in letters, but you will be raising the children alone until your husband is released from prison. Single parenting is challenging, but it has its rewards also. Try to locate other single parents with whom you can share ideas, problems, solutions, and baby-sitting duties. You are not alone.

While most single mothers carry extra emotional and physical burdens, those with a husband in prison must also overcome negative social stigmas. Therefore, it is essential to develop a core of personal strength and inner confidence—self-esteem.

Developing Self-esteem

Pride and respect in one's self denotes self-esteem. Self-esteem gives you a core of inner balance, even when the world around you seems to be swirling off center.

As the wife of an inmate, you may feel that you should hang your head in shame for what your husband did, but you need to separate yourself from your husband's mistakes. You have no control over your husband's illegal actions. Accept yourself as a person separate from your husband with distinctive actions and make a commitment to yourself to take charge of your future. Build your self-esteem on *your* actions and deeds. Walk with your head up and shoulders back to let others know that you respect yourself.

How do you develop self-esteem after your husband has been imprisoned for breaking the law? How do you develop self-esteem when you are nearly financially destitute, feel socially outcast , and emotionally drained? Everyone, even the most successful people in the world, experience failure and disappointment. However, emotionally well-balanced people have learned to accept these losses and disappointments by growing through the pain and gaining new strength for the next task. Just as baseball games are won with one pitch, one hit, and one run at a time, life's challenges are met and overcome one day at a time.

~**Positive Thinking and Affirmations:** Build your self-esteem by developing positive thinking. Imagine that you are suceeding each day in little ways and that the future is going to bring you new and brighter opportunities. Focus on the day at hand, the issues at hand, and on making the most of what you have. Everyone faces problems in their daily lives. Stop believing that your problems are worse than anyone else's. And, begin believing that you are working to solve your problems.

Claim this truth: Within yourself, you have what it takes to overcome your problems. You can learn from this situation. You can become a better person from this struggle. Begin your days with positive affirmations or short sayings that remind you of the good in yourself and in your life:

- I am worthy of a happy life.

- I am worthy of a happy family.

- I am a loving person.

- I am a loving mother.

- Good things are coming my way.

- Every day, in every way, things are getting better and better.

Each morning think about what you have to be grateful for. Energy follows thought. Concentrating on positive thoughts will heighten your sense of the good things around you.

~**Exercise:** Make regular exercise a part of your weekly schedule. Try walking around the block, swimming, playing badminton or basketball, or riding a bike with your children. Exercise does not need to be rigorous. Routine exercise of any kind will further your sense of self-esteem. Taking care of your body and your physical health promotes a sense of well-being and control.

~**Friends:** Pursue friendships with people who are positive and who exemplify the characteristics you are striving to develop in yourself. Look for people who have a positive outlook towards life and take responsibility for their actions. Avoid people who focus on the past and don't support your efforts toward positive change.

~**Journal Writing:** You don't have to be a writer to reap the benefits of journal writing. A journal is a place to explore your emotions and learn more about yourself. Buy an inexpensive notebook to serve as your journal, then find a private place to keep it. Remember that what you write is for your eyes only, and plan to write in your journal during times of the day when you are alone.

Journal writing begins with simple exercises that explore the "stuff" of your inner and outer life. Your journal will support your work towards building self-esteem and a sense of control over your present life. Journal work will also help you develop acceptance towards your past and a sense of hope for your future.

~**Self Praise:** Rejoice in your successes. Cheer on each small, but successful step you take—getting through another day, helping the children through homework, walking briskly around the block, paying another bill, or reading and laughing with your children before bed. These are positive accomplishments. Applaud yourself for surviving. Later, as you strengthen your self-esteem and confidence, your accomplishments will become larger. But, don't expect big changes overnight. Remember: take one day at a time.

Developing Time Management Skills

If you have not been an organized parent before, now is the time to begin organizing your family's life. The daily or weekly help of a relative or friend will lighten your load some, but you will find that you have less time and more responsibilities while fulfilling the role of a single parent.

Careful management of your time will give you more freedom in which to enjoy your children. Sit down at the beginning of each week and write a list of tasks, errands, and responsibilities on a calendar. As each task is finished, check it off and feel a sense of accomplishment. If you are unable to complete everything on your schedule, don't fret. Place unfinished tasks on the top of the next week's schedule and do them first. Don't forget to make time for some fun in your schedule. When you know what you have to do in a given week, you will feel in control of your life.

Developing Self-esteem in Children

Children are likely to live up to what you believe in them.
—Lady Bird Johnson

In a society where so much emphasis is placed upon image, and a family's social status is most often determined by the father's job, children of a convicted felon are facing a distinct disadvantage. Therefore, children of inmates can very easily assume a negative self-image.

It is your job as a single parent to help your children prepare for the world they must face each day at school and at play. Statistics from the U.S. Bureau of Prisons indicate that children of an incarcerated parent are <u>six times</u> more likely to end up in prison than other children. This statistic is frightening; therefore, it is up to you to keep your children from becoming a part of this statistic. Do not allow your children to fall into the stereotype phrased as such: "That poor kid will never amount to anything because his father is in prison." Instead, help your children develop the attitude that they can accomplish as much, if not more, in school and life in spite of the fact that they have a parent in prison.

Children's self-esteem is developed much the same as an adult; yet, children will first look to a parent as a positive role model. As a parent develops self-esteem, it will be easier for children to do the same. Helping children develop self-esteem begins with an underlying foundation of unconditional love— love with no strings attached. This does not mean you will never discipline your children or express your anger when they misbehave or engage in destructive activities; rather, it means that you will love your children regardless of their behavior. Unconditional love is the largest commitment you can make to your children. Let them know that no matter how busy you are, their health and happiness are your first priority. Encourage your children to communicate with you. Let them know that you want to listen to all of their feelings and confusions about their parent's incarceration and, indeed, about all aspects of their lives. Make time to be alone with each child on a regular basis so that he or she can continue to talk about thoughts and feelings.

Your children may experience mood swings, which alternate between missing their incarcerated parent and feeling angry towards him. Let children know that these emotional swings are normal. Tell them it's okay to be confused about prison and about their parent. Let them know that you have these same shifts in feeling and attitude, which are a part of the natural grieving process.

If a young child is having trouble vocalizing his hurt, help by initiating conversations directed at the problems. Helpful questions to ask: It's difficult having daddy gone right now, isn't it? What do you miss the most? Sometimes I just don't know how to explain where daddy is to my friends. Do you ever feel that way? These conversations can take place while doing household chores together or while sharing a meal. Sometimes the unscheduled "quality times" can be the best.

Today, a typical American home may easily be compared to a train station. Each member of the home passes through the train station for brief stops and refueling, and then everyone hurries back out in different directions. This was certainly an accurate description of our house, especially as my boys got older. One way to slow the trains down a little is to make an attempt to have everyone in your family sit down to dinner together each night of the week. Encourage conversation about the day's activities. Family support can be your greatest strength through difficult times. "Dinnertime is of more significance to child development than playtime, school, and story time." This was revealed by following sixty-five families over an eight year period, reports FOCUS ON THE FAMILY, November 2000.

Your children's self-esteem will be bolstered by their knowledge that they can handle unknown situations. Maybe they are worried about you leaving them. Assure them you have no intentions of going anywhere. But also give them the tools they need to handle an emergency alone:

- Post emergency phone numbers on your refrigerator or near the phone. Explain the significance of each number.

- Identify neighbors or family members your children can go to or call if they are alone and need help.

- Review your procedures regarding strangers, phone calls, fires, cooking, playing outside, and visiting friends. Have your children express any fears they may have, and work through your family policy regarding these fears until the children are comfortable with each policy. Never refer to your children's fears as unrealistic.

Another way to help in your children's self-esteem development is to assign your children individual tasks. Not only does this make housework easier for you, but it gives the children the opportunity to complete an assignment successfully. Chores must be geared to children's ages and skill levels. Don't give children too much to do, as you don't want them to fail. But don't underestimate children's abilities either. Establish rules and rewards around the chores, and be sure to give praise for a job well done. Let the children know how much their work helps the family unit run smoothly. Moreover, children like to succeed. Accomplishment, praise, and security help develop self-esteem. Therefore, remember to tell your children that you love them every day. Show them with a hug and a kiss. Tell them, "You're special. I love you."

Children and Chores

Since household chores are not the highlight of any child's day, I built incentives into my children's chores so that they didn't correlate daily or weekend tasks with punishment.

When my boys were very young, I inserted a counting game into the task of picking up stray toys and clothes. Each boy was given a basket and his responsibility was to pick up ten stray items and count each item out loud while putting them in his basket. This game encouraged the boys to learn their numbers and keep the house tidy. Moreover, I often expanded the rules by offering a reward to the boy who picked up ten items the fastest and returned them to their appropriate places. And, on Fridays I ordered pizza as soon as the house was cleaned. Needless to say, the boys were very helpful on Fridays.

In addition to incentive-based chores, I also established house rules that we all had to adhere to in order to maintain order and discipline in the household.

1. Each person in the house had to make his bed before anyone was allowed to leave the house. Occasionally, we were late for school at the beginning of a school year. But as soon as the boys realized that we wouldn't leave the house until their beds were made, they quickly adhered to the rule. And, since I refused to write an excuse for them if they were late for school, they learned to take responsibility for their actions.

2. All dirty clothes were to be placed in the laundry basket or they didn't get washed. Each of the boys went through phases of forgetting to give me their dirty clothes; however, after wearing dirty clothes for a day or two, they soon stopped forgetting to bring me their clothes that needed washing.

3. All toys needed to be picked up. If I discovered toys that were not put away, I gave the boys a warning. If the toys were not picked up after the warning, I picked them up and placed them into a box that was off limits to them. Sometimes I returned the toys in a few weeks and sometimes not at all, which encouraged the boys to pick up their toys routinely.

4. Everyone was expected to clear the dishes from the table. I'll never forget when my youngest son was eight-teen-months-old and he proudly carried his plate to the kitchen sink while dragging his oxygen cord behind him. I realized that children can be taught to accomplish chores at a very young age.

5. Yard work was always a family event. My oldest son usually mowed the grass, (beginning at age eight), while the rest of us pulled weeds, raked leaves, and trimmed bushes.

6. Homework was not optional. I required the boys to complete their homework at the dining room table, where I joined them to offer help when needed.

7. When the boys got older, I gave each of them an alarm clock so that they were responsible for meeting the car pool and arriving at school on time.

8. I taught the boys how to peel potatoes and carrots, make a salad, barbeque on a grill, set the table, and bake bread. Once they got older they thanked me for those skills. Children are never too young to start learning how to help out in the kitchen.

9. Once the boys reached age twelve, I taught them how to launder their clothing.

10. The boys were given small allowances each week. Although my finances were lean, I wanted my boys to understand the importance of earning and saving money.

Organizing a household based on routine, rules, and a reward system helps maintain an orderly structure and encourages the family to work as a team.

Children and Imprisoned Parents: Keeping the Love Alive
Your children are going to follow your lead in regard to

their relationship with their imprisoned parent. Your ability to demonstrate your continued love and caring to your imprisoned spouse will give your children permission to reveal their love and caring also.

If you are still married and intend your marriage to survive the time apart, communicate that to your children. They need reassurance about your continued love for your spouse, the reasons you are willing to live alone during this time of separation, and your plans to rebuild your marriage after your spouse is released from prison.

Phone Calls From Prison: Children

Give children minutes alone on the phone with the imprisoned parent. Support their relationship with the parent in prison and help them to keep the lines of love and communication open via phone calls. Children need to know that even though their parent has been taken away it does not mean that they have stopped loving them.

Keep a list of those things you want to share about the children. Sharing little things such as a good grade on a test or learning how to ride a bike keeps the prisoner in touch with the daily life of his children. If a child wants to tell an imprisoned parent about something trivial he or she did five minutes ago, let them.

Phone Calls from Prison: Spouse

In the first few months, a wife may have a great deal of anger towards her incarcerated husband. And, unfortunately, phone calls may become a source of venting frustration.

Although it is vital that you tell your imprisoned spouse what is on your mind, there are a few guidelines you can follow to make phone calls more productive and satisfying. Be organized. Write down your feelings prior to the phone call in order to address all of your current concerns. Keep this list where you can find it when the inmate calls. Calls are usually brief; so, make the most of them. Be efficient, but also make an effort to include the positive parts of your life. Ask your spouse for advice about situations you are facing alone. Ask him to think about future decisions you must make, giving his response at a later date. You want him to recognize the importance of your partnership during his absence. Also, give each child a few minutes to talk. Set a timer so that everyone knows when his or her time is up. And, if possible, avoid angry confrontations over the phone. A screaming match will only leave you more frustrated than before he called. Leave the big issues for letters and for prison visits. Let your anger unroll in your journal notebook, or keep a list of those issues you want to talk about with him when you visit the prison.

Phone calls from prison are a vehicle you can use to keep a loved one in touch with ordinary family life. Ask your loved one to listen and offer the same in return. Be respectful of one another over the phone. You will not solve your big problems or disagreements in a ten minute phone call, so don't try.

Marriage, Divorce, and Sexuality

You are probably going to question your marriage many times throughout your spouse's incarceration. Although you are a married woman, you have none of the benefits married women enjoy, including the financial, emotional, and physical support of a husband. You may have lost respect for your spouse and question why you are still married. You may think about dating. Therefore, you have to weigh your love for your spouse with your present feelings and prospects. You must also understand that your marriage may never be the same even after he returns from prison.

Don't make hasty decisions regarding your marriage.

Share your doubts and confusions with a good friend, counselor, pastor, or priest. It is okay to feel uncertain about your future. Let the feelings surface; one day you may want to remain married and the next day you want out. Just take your feelings a day at a time. Have confidence that you will make the right decision in the future. Remember: your emotions may change enormously from day to day; so, don't make a decision about your marriage based on one or two days of anger or bitterness.

The Social Life of an Inmate's Wife

Your social life is going to change when your husband goes to prison. You are no longer part of a couple, yet you are not single either. Where do you fit?

Seek out friends with whom you can share simple pleasures like a movie or a cup of coffee before the children come home for dinner. Accept offers from friends and co-workers to socialize together as a group. Invite friends to your house for dinner and conversation. Even if your friends are married, there are many opportunities for social contact and exchange that do not revolve around couples. Participate in school functions, church activities, craft classes, or community events where people that are married or single are welcomed. Allow yourself to interact with adults without feeling out of place. Our society is full of single parent households. You are not alone.

The Sexual Life of the Inmate's Wife

You have lost your closest companion, emotionally and sexually. The length of your loved one's prison sentence, the level of trust and commitment you have shared with him in the past, and your own values are going to determine what you do and don't do while your husband is imprisoned.

You must consider your children as well as yourself. Has your marriage been healthy or troubled? Perhaps you should seek a support group. Consult your priest, rabbi, or minister for guidance reflective of your religious affiliation and spiritual beliefs. Much of the emptiness you feel might be eased through creative pursuits, and your sense of isolation may be lessened through your relationships with friends and with your family.

Some prisons allow conjugal visits; however, the federal prison where my husband was incarcerated did not allow them. In general, a prison that does allow conjugal visits doles them out as a reward for good behavior or for an impeccable record. If you are given permission to engage in sexual activity with your spouse during a prison visit, use protection, as hepatitis C is prevalent in many prisons.

Mistakes are the portals of discovery.

—James Joyce

8

For Parents, Siblings, and Friends

When someone close to you commits a crime that places him in prison, you may feel responsible for his behavior and betrayed at the same time. But, the fact remains that once a person is an adult he is responsible for his actions. People are influenced by peer pressure, alcohol, drugs, and money problems to commit crimes. Relatives and close friends can try to affect an individual's behavior; but, ultimately, the caregivers cannot live the prisoner's life for him.

Let your guilt go! Stop the mental narrative that says, "If only I had....." or "I should have....." This sort of thinking will only make you more frustrated and depressed. Your loved one doesn't need your self-recriminations and guilt. He needs your attention focused on the present, not the past.

Share your feelings. If your relationship with an imprisoned family member has been less than close for a few years, perhaps it is time to renew your relationship. It may be easiest or safest to start by writing a letter in which you can say what you feel without interruption. Be honest as you share your feelings. Express your hope that you can become closer, even while he is in prison. Prison allows time for reflection. Give your loved one positive topics to examine. The renewal of family relationships is a great beginning.

Whether or not you have forgiven your loved one, personal contact will be helpful for all. Families are often torn apart when a member is sentenced to prison. Brothers, sisters, fathers, or mothers may start the blame game and begin quarreling. Avoid taking sides and encourage the family to stop finding fault. Now is the time to work together and rebuild the family.

Keep the lines of communication open no matter how angry, disappointed, or embarrassed you may feel towards the incarcerated loved one. Stay in touch with each other through letters, phone calls, or prison visits if appropriate. Make a vow to him and to yourself that you are going to maintain an open heart. Make a commitment to do whatever it takes to heal the family. Be honest. Tell your incarcerated family member or friend how his actions have made you feel. Allow him space to be honest with you. Listen to his side of the story. Only after you both have frankly expressed your emotions can you go forward in a better relationship.

Your loved one needs you now more than ever before. Recognize your importance to him, even if he cannot reciprocate the feelings. Let him know that he is not forgotten and that his welfare is important to you.

Keeping an Incarcerated Loved One in the Family Circle

You can increase an inmate's sense of belonging to the family by sharing daily life in your letters to him. Things you may think are too trivial or unimportant may be just what an inmate longs for. Share everything including incidents at work, school activities, athletic events, weather, or community events. Take pictures of your world. Send newspaper clippings and photos of trips, places, people, holidays, and other gatherings. Clip articles in newspapers and magazines that pertain to a prisoner's career or interests. Find out if the prison will allow you to send your loved one old magazines. If permitted, mail such items at book rate. Write a separate letter stating what magazines you have included in the package and the date you mailed the package. This letter then informs the inmate of the contents and confirms what you sent.

If the inmate's calls are collect, and if you can afford to cover the cost of the calls, you may suggest that he call you from prison whenever possible. Talk about everyday affairs and events. Begin by sharing what you did that day, who you saw, and what you thought about. You may feel uncomfortable at first, but you will find that simple gestures of friendship, support, and sincere communication will relax both of you.

All calls made from a prison are recorded, monitored by a correctional officer, or both. Be sure that whatever you say on the phone you would feel comfortable hearing again in a room full of people. Do not discuss illegal activities.

For the Parents Reaching Out to an Inmate's Family: How Much is Enough?

As the parents or in-laws of a prisoner, you will soon have to decide how much financial, emotional, and physical help you can offer your son's family. While your son or son-in-law is in prison, the loss of his earnings can be devastating to his wife. Rather quickly, you will need to decide if you can help in the form of childcare or financial aid. Evaluate your decisions before you take action. Don't try to alleviate an old guilt towards your son or son-in-law by rescuing his family if you are not capable of fulfilling the commitment. Base your offer of aid and support on what is really best for you and for your extended family.

All family members must work together in understanding their emotions and stresses. The inmate's family must stop blaming the past failures. The individual family members of an inmate need to adopt a positive attitude that can offer hope to the loved one in prison and those left at home. By doing this, they can find better solutions for the present and the future.

And in the end, it's not the years in your life that count; it's the life in your years.

—Abraham Lincoln

9

Prison Visits

Before you Go

Before you embark on your first visit to a prison, be certain you and the inmate have completed all appropriate paperwork required by the institution.

Inmate's Visitor List

An inmate is allowed to place a limited number of people (usually ten) on his visitor list. Immediate family—wife and children—are classified as one of the ten. For your name to be on the visitor list, the inmate must have completed the official information sheet listing visitor's names, ages, addresses, and relationship to the inmate.

For those seeking visitor privileges who are not immediate family, a questionnaire is usually mailed from the prison to that individual. This form must be filled out and mailed back to the institution. Allow several days for mailing and processing. If you are not certain that your name is on the visitor list, have the inmate check with his prison counselor before you plan to visit. Unless your name is on the inmate's visitor list there is little chance you will be allowed to visit. Exceptions to this rule are made for clergy and attorneys.

The Prison Visit

The first visit will probably be the most difficult. You will need to learn the location of the restricted parking lot, where and how to enter the prison, and what is expected of you. You will not know any of the correctional officers' procedures or expectations. Correctional officers and staff can be courteous and friendly, or they can be rude and temperamental. During your first prison visit be patient with yourself and others.

Try to plan your first prison visit as soon as possible. Seeing your spouse's living conditions will probably help you adjust more quickly to the separation.

~Who will go?

Your children have probably imagined all sorts of things about their parent's prison life. Television and movies create a sense of horror behind bars, which may cause your children to worry about their parent. It is important to take your children on the first visit so that they can put aside frightening scenarios about prison life.

Trip List

~**Transportation** If you have a car and will be driving yourself, make sure the car is in good working order. If someone else will be driving, organize your plans with him or her. Fill up the gas tank and check the oil the day before departure.

~**Directions** If you must travel to a new city, obtain a map and directions before the day of the trip. Look them over and familiarize yourself with your travel route.

~**Overnight Accommodations** If you will be traveling overnight, arrange hotel accommodations before you leave. If you will be staying with friends, make sure they know when you will be arriving. If you prefer to stay in a hotel near the prison, call a local travel agent and ask for the various hotel rates of your destination city. The travel agent can arrange a hotel reservation within your budget. If you arrive without a reservation and there is not a room available at the cost you expected, tell them you will look somewhere else unless they negotiate the price of the room.

Choose comfortable clothes for your travel and visit. Pack several items of clothing in case the air conditioning or heat in the hotel or prison visiting room is not adequate. Take clothes that are appropriate for the visit. Women will not be allowed to visit in the prison if they are wearing shorts, sexy or provocative clothing, lack undergarments, or any clothing viewed as offensive to the correctional officer.

~**Packing for Children** Pack clothes that are easy to care for and comfortable for hours of wear in the car, in the prison waiting room, and perhaps at a playground. Do not over-dress your children. Let them wear clothes they are comfortable in.

~**Pack your car the night before** Place overnight bags and non-perishable food in the car the night before your trip to avoid a late start. Take favorite snack foods, canned or boxed juices, soft drinks, and a packed lunch to avoid expensive snacks and meals at fast food restaurants. Take games, crayons, paper, coloring books, and playing cards that will make the trip more enjoyable for your children and you. If you don't have a tape deck or CD player in your car, take along a portable unit so that your children can listen to tapes of music or books. Make sure you carry enough cash for gas, food, and lodging. If you have a credit card, take it. Also take change, especially quarters, as most prison vending machines require quarters. Generally, visitors are not allowed to take dollar bills into the visiting area.

~**Make the Most of Your Trip** Even if you are on a very tight budget, make your trip to the prison a special time with your family or for yourself. When planning the trip, find out if there are any landmarks or special stops between your home and your destination. Parks or historic sites make lovely picnic places. Most towns have a public playground, park, or schoolyard where you can stop to stretch your legs and enjoy a picnic. A local shopping mall can provide an air-conditioned respite from a hot car. Use the restrooms and walk the length of the mall for exercise. Enjoy your trip. Try not to worry about the money you must spend to make this trip. You need to visit your loved one, so try to enjoy the journey.

Prison Pre-registration

Upon arrival at the prison, you will be asked to fill out a special visitor form and present a photo identification card. Make sure you have brought one along, as I have seen visitors not allowed to visit because they had forgotten their picture I.D. Your name and your children's names will then be checked against the inmate's visitors list.

The category of the institution will determine the level of security that will surround your visit. The following are common procedures during a prison visit:

• You will probably be scanned by metal detectors.

• Personal belongings, including a purse, will probably be temporarily removed from your being and secured in a locked area.

• Many institutions have dogs that patrol the parking lots. Your car may be searched.

• You may be assigned seats in numbered chairs.

• Correctional officers will probably remain nearby during your entire visit.

• Visits are often recorded on television monitors.

• A strip search is unusual, but may be required of you and/or your children. Prepare your children for this possibility so that they are not fearful or upset by any prison procedure they may encounter. If a strip search is requested, you do have the right to refuse, but you will then have to leave the institution. When you refuse the strip search and leave, your actions will be recorded in the inmate's file. You may be refused further visitation rights. If you agree to the strip search, you will be asked to sign a consent form before the search takes place.

• Assume that babies in diapers will be searched.

Contraband in Prison

Contraband may include drugs, medicine, alcohol, cash, clothing, jewelry, photos, magazines, books, or items not authorized by the prison. Never bring contraband to the prison. If you bring contraband to the prison, not only will you jeopardize the inmate, but you will put yourself at risk. Anyone caught with contraband may be detained and turned over to law enforcement authorities. In addition, your visitation rights will probably be revoked.

Only after you have been approved for admittance will the inmate be called. Allow plenty of time for pre-registration and admittance procedures; this can be very time consuming. Also, if you arrive at the prison during the inmate count, expect to wait up to an hour before the inmate is released to the visiting area.

Special Rules

Before you visit the prison, find out what rules apply to visitors. For instance, there are rules regarding food. Very few institutions will allow you to bring in food, but some prisons will allow you to order meals that can be delivered from a local restaurant. If they do permit this, you will have to order through the prison. Find out what the institution's policy is about ordering food. Sometimes I was allowed to order pizza from a local restaurant. I filled out an order form, paid for the pizza in advance, and our order was called in to the restaurant by a staff member of the institution. This was a real treat for us the few times it was allowed.

If you need to breast feed your baby while visiting, notify a guard. He may arrange a private room for this purpose. I breast fed my youngest son on our first two visits without incident. On our third visit, a corrections officer rushed over to me in the visiting room and informed me that I wasn't allowed to nurse my baby in there, which upset all of us. I was told I would have to go to a private area, which greatly reduced my time available to visit with my husband. In time, the officers finally let our whole family go into the private room while I nursed the baby.

I believe the officers finally showed some compassion to us because I didn't complain or cause any problems when I was told I had to leave the visiting area; moreover, I tidied up the private room before leaving. Correctional officers are people who work in a difficult environment and experience rude and unpredictable people on a daily basis. Therefore, always be courteous to the correctional officers. Don't question their authority or decisions regarding you and your children. If correctional officers make you angry, don't show it. You are on their turf and must follow their rules.

Visiting Time with the Inmate

When you take children to visit their father, allow at least fifteen minutes of private time for each child to spend with his father. It will call for a lot of patience on the part of everyone, including you, but ultimately your visit will be more productive if everyone is given a special allowance of visiting time. This may involve simply moving to another area of the visiting room to find privacy.

When it is your turn alone with your spouse, you may find yourself suddenly overwhelmed by conflicting emotions. After the elation of seeing your husband again, you may find that you will fall right back into the anger you felt the day he was arrested. It's okay. Don't be surprised by confusing bursts of emotions. Discuss your feelings. Share with him what it is like living alone. Let him know how hard it is to be a single parent, work, pay bills, and go to the welfare office. You don't need to feel guilty if you are angry or sad. A prison visit is not about pretending that everything on the outside is fine. A prison visit is about honest communication.

If you are traveling a long distance, try to visit the prison for two days. Often the first day will be devoted almost entirely to an inmate's catching up with the children. By the second day, the children are usually less interested in visiting with their imprisoned parent, leaving you more time with your spouse.

The Inmate and Children: Discipline

Prior to the visit, arrange guidelines for you and your spouse to follow regarding your children's discipline. It is important that the imprisoned spouse maintain a parental role. He must continue to be co-disciplinarian with his children even while in prison. If children need scolding or redirection during the visit, it must not fall entirely on the parent who has brought them and lives with them. Remind the incarcerated parent that his duties and responsibilities to the children have not changed.

Hospitality Centers

Some prisons may have hospitality centers near them. The hospitality centers that I am familiar with are similar to an elementary school classroom. They have trained staff that supervise children while a spouse or family member visits the inmate. The centers are separate buildings outside the grounds of the prison, wherein the children do not have to enter the prison or go through any prison security. The centers generally offer outdoor play, crafts, books, TV, rest areas, and snacks.

In addition, hospitality centers often provide a "clothing closet" for visitors that are not dressed appropriately for a prison visit. Many visitors don't realize the strict policies most prisons have regarding dress. For example, all adult female visitors must wear undergarments. Shorts are not permitted, nor is "sexy" clothing. Often it is the correctional officer on duty that determines what type of clothing is acceptable.

After the Visit: Alone Again

Re-enter the world outside the prison slowly. Expect to grieve for a day or two after the visit. Rely on the inner strength that has brought you through other tough times. Establish your sense of solidarity and balance by talking with a good friend or counselor. Write about your visit and the ensuing emotions in your journal. And, keep busy with your job or the chores at hand.

Holidays: Stay Home or Visit Prison?

The best things you can give children, next to good habits, are good memories.

—Sydney J. Harris

Holidays can present a dilemma for families of inmates. You may want to be with your imprisoned loved one; and, you know the prisoner wants to be with his family and children. Even so, there are many reasons for not visiting the prison over the holiday unless you live in the same city where he is incarcerated.

Your family deserves special observances of favorite family traditions. Children need holidays that are spent with parents, grandparents, and good friends in an atmosphere of love and fun. Yet, the prison atmosphere will never be one of loving support. No matter what day of the year it is, the prison is going to feel the same: confining, bleak, and heartless. Therefore, why not allow your children and family members to spend holidays at home where they can celebrate in a manner they will treasure all their lives? Even with the best intentions, a holiday spent in a prison visitation room is a cruel sentence for children and loved ones.

I made sure that my sons and I were always home for Christmas Eve, Christmas Day, and Easter. If my boys had spent every Christmas Eve for six years of their young lives in a prison visiting room, I would not have been able to teach them holiday traditions, and they would have missed out on special congregational events. Since a prison visiting room looks the same on Christmas Eve as it does any other day of the week, give your children positive memories of holidays that they will be able to share with their families in the years ahead.

~Holidays for the Inmate

Holidays are usually the only time a prison will provide special meals and activities. There may be a turkey dinner served for Thanksgiving and softball tournaments planned for the Fourth of July. If an inmate has visitors, he may have to miss out on the only festivities ever offered to inmates. I recommend checking with your spouse to see if he wishes to participate in prison activities over holidays instead of receiving visitors.

~Holiday Options

For many people, holidays are the only days off from work. And with children out of school, holidays provide the rare opportunity for most families to visit a loved one in prison without missing work or academic obligations. Yet, family members may not wish to devote their entire holiday to a prison visit. If possible, stay home with family and friends on the actual holiday, and then plan your visit to the prison for the day after or the day before the holiday.

Many prisons have special visiting hours during holiday weekends. Find out the prison schedule on and around holiday events. Plan your holiday so that everyone in the family is taken into account. Do not feel guilty if you choose to stay home. Holidays provide valuable time for families to get together and enjoy one another. Your family deserves special days and family traditions at home.

Disadvantages of Living Close to the Prison

Living near the prison where your loved one is incarcerated can make prison visits much easier and certainly less costly. But there are also hardships that come with living in close proximity to the prison. Most institutions limit visiting to some degree, but with careful scheduling, family visits to the prison can be made almost every weekend. At first this may calm a family's separation anxiety with their imprisoned loved one and vice versa. However, frequent visits can create expectation on the part of the inmate. This expectation may quickly become a problem for everyone. After the first month, family members may find that they need to return to their own lives. They may begin to yearn for other activities, not wishing to sit out their weekends in a prison visitation room. A loved one's prison sentence should not become a prison sentence for the entire family. Don't ever force children to spend a Saturday afternoon sitting in a prison visiting room if they don't want to be there.

You may feel guilty when you want to attend your children's athletic events or a friend's barbecue rather than spend a Saturday at the prison. Set the guilt aside. Some weekends, you could visit your husband alone, leaving your children to enjoy activities with friends. And, perhaps one weekend a month you could plan events for your family outside of the prison. Do not apologize for your life outside of the prison. You did not break the law and place your spouse in prison. Rather, you are living alone and paying the price for his mistake in several ways every day of your life. Don't burden yourself with guilt about the few pleasures that come your way. Enjoy yourself. Take the children to birthday parties and school or congregational activities. Be with your friends. Life continues on the outside and you must be a part of it.

Note: If you are considering relocating in order to live near the prison where your spouse is incarcerated, please consider the hardships you may endure by doing so. A new city may leave you and your children void of friends, family, and established medical practitioners. Additionally, you will be faced with several relocation charges, such as moving transportation, utility and phone deposits, and new home costs.

Taking Photos Behind Bars

You will find that some prisons allow photographs to be taken at specified times and places, but find out what the rules are. In my experience, the prison provided the camera and film and my husband paid for the photo through his commissary account. I was not allowed to bring my camera into the prison.

I recommend that you take pictures of your family whenever possible. I used a current family photo each year for my Christmas cards, and throughout the year I made copies of our family "prison portraits" and sent them to relatives and friends. The photograph tells friends and family that you are still together and that you are surviving this difficult time in your lives. Be proud of your family. You are survivors!

Courage is fear holding on a minute longer.
—George S. Patton

10

My Most Memorable Visit

I made approximately fifty visits to my husband in prison, but my second visit stands as the most memorable. The boys were very young—ages eight, six, three, and eighteen months. And, not only did that make for a boisterous carload, but my baby was reliant on an oxygen tank and regular breast feedings.

After rising at 5:00 AM, filling my baby's oxygen tank, and dressing the boys, we headed out for our second prison visit. The four hour drive totally wore me out. Petty bickering, fist-fights, intervals of breastfeeding, and, perhaps, general uneasiness about the visit made us all edgy and uptight. I laugh now, because we must have looked like a "Family Circus" cartoon when we finally arrived at the prison. The two older boys were fighting, and my baby was hungry and screaming. We stepped into the scorching heat of midmorning in the desert still grumpy.

After tackling the stroller and oxygen tank, we were ready to face the uphill climb to the prison. I realized I would have a very difficult time negotiating the stroller, balancing the oxygen, and climbing the steps, so I opted for the handicapped path, which was void of steps. When we reached the entrance, the corrections officer came out and quickly told me that I was not allowed to be in that area. I calmly tried to explain that my baby was on oxygen and that maneuvering the stairs would be very difficult, all things considered. It was only after my lengthy explanation that he seemed to finally notice the oxygen tank. He looked at me and the boys and grumbled something under his breath before allowing us inside and then disappearing.

The rest of the visit was basically uneventful and routine. Visiting hours ended at 3:00 PM, so we said our good-byes and headed back to the car. By then, it was 106 degrees outside, so we quickly hurried to the car. I knew I would have to get home as soon as possible, because my baby's portable oxygen supply was being depleted. As we reached the car, I started searching for my keys, but they were not where I usually kept them. We were quickly becoming overheated and frustrated. After dumping the contents of my purse onto the hood of the car and not finding the keys, I glanced into the interior of the car. The keys were dangling from the ignition. By that time all the other visitors had left, and the five of us were stranded in the deserted parking lot. I was so angry with myself that tears stung my eyes as I stuffed everything back into my purse. The boys, sensing something was wrong, became quiet. I told them where the keys were and that we would have to go back to the prison. Trudging back up the sidewalk to the side entrance of the visitor's building, I expected trouble. Sure enough, a corrections officer came out and gruffly told me I had to leave because visiting hours were over and by remaining on the property I was breaking the rules. I told him that I had locked my keys in the car and politely asked him if I could make a phone call from inside the prison. He paused just long enough for me to fear that perhaps he would leave us stranded. In an angry tone, he told me that I could use the phone. I think he was afraid he would get in trouble by helping me, but he eventually let us into the coolness of the air conditioned building.

Meanwhile, my husband had been watching this scenario from a hill that overlooked the parking lot. When he saw us head back to the visiting area, he realized we had a problem, so he entered the visitor's building at the far end. Before we could say anything to him, a corrections officer suddenly appeared, took him by the arms, and hauled him away. Now his situation added to my worry, as I did not know if they would take him to "the hole" or punish him in some way.

Finally, the corrections officer calmed down enough for me to quietly ask again if I could use the phone. By this time my baby was hungry and crying, and the boys were upset. The corrections officer looked at us and realized that he would not get any peace until we were out of there. He led us to a small office and roughly pushed a phone towards me. Although I am a member of AAA, I didn't have their phone number handy; so, I fearfully looked up at him and meekly asked if I could borrow a phone book. He glared at me before tossing the yellow pages in my direction. Ultimately, the stress of the situation, the heat, my anger at myself, and my need to get my baby home for oxygen caused me to break down into tears. As soon as the AAA dispatcher spoke to me, I began sobbing out of control. The more I tried to talk, the harder I cried. I gently felt the receiver being taken out of my hand. To my amazement, the corrections officer was talking to the dispatcher and telling her my problem and car location. His voice had softened. He hung up and we both just looked at each other. Maybe he realized this was not any fun for me either. Maybe I reminded him of his wife, sister, or moth-

er. Maybe he realized that the sooner I got out of there, the easier life would be for him. At any rate, his demeanor changed, and
he became nicer to us.

He was not nice enough, however, to let us wait inside
the air-conditioned building; so, back out to the 106 degree heat
we went. We all were very subdued at this point. We were worn
out. We had experienced a side of prison life first hand that was
not pleasant. My heart ached for all six of us, and for the future
years that would force us to be impacted by the prison system.
My husband had only been in prison for a few months, and he
had a fifteen year sentence ahead of him.

We must have been a pitiful sight sitting on the curb near
my car. We waited forty-five minutes for the AAA service man to
show up, but waited only twelve seconds for him to open the car
door and hand me my keys. The thought of having been twelve
seconds away from freedom prompted more tears. I loaded up
the boys, diaper bag, and oxygen and started to drive away.
Suddenly, one of the boys spotted my husband on the hill wav-
ing to us, which let us know that he was okay and not detained.
Through the tears I waved back. It was a long trip home and I
often had trouble seeing the road through my tears. The boys
were unusually quiet and kept trying to comfort me. But, we all
survived.

My advice to you is this: join AAA or an emergency road
service; the peace of mind it provides is well worth the cost.
Also, purchase a metal key box from an auto parts store. The
back side of this key box serves as a magnet, which will enable
you to hide a spare key in the box and place it under your car.

Resolve to be a master of change rather than a victim of change.
—Brian Tracy

11

Stretching a Dollar

The loss of your husband's income may lead to financial hardship. Such was my experience; yet, it was only through trial and error that I learned how to manage a household on less money than was required to support four boys and myself.

Several months after my husband was imprisoned, my financial situation went from questionable to dire. Although my husband and I had always kept two freezers packed with food, my boys and I were moving through the supplies steadily without replenishing them. After one freezer was emptied, I unplugged it and then did the same with the second freezer. Since I was desperate for money, I held a yard sale and sold one of the freezers and whatever household belongings I could do without. However, at ten cents on the dollar, I didn't profit much from the sale. Desperate for a solution, I scanned the classified ads for a job, but there were no environments in which I could bring my baby, who required forced oxygen and breast-feeding. And, I wasn't able hire a babysitter, because I didn't have enough money after the IRS seized our checking and savings accounts, which essentially left me penniless.

Swallowing my pride, I decided to seek government assistance. I headed to the local food stamp office nicely dressed, baby and oxygen tank in tow. As soon as I arrived at the reception desk, the receptionist inquired if I was there to apply for the job opening. Humiliated, I explained that I needed to apply for food stamps. Her demeanor abruptly shifted from pleasant to abrasive as she pointed to a sea of people and uttered, "Get in line." After reaching the end of the line, my baby and I became instantly entrenched in a pall of cigarette smoke. Although I politely pointed out my baby's oxygen tank, not to mention my baby, and requested that the smokers be cautious of open flames when lighting their cigarettes, most of the people were indifferent to my plea. In fact, as an act of defiance, one man blew smoke directly at my baby and me. Tears stung my eyes and I wanted to run back home, but I was determined to find a way to feed my sons.

So, after a two-hour wait, a representative finally called me into her office. Although I was surprised to see my former ski patrol co-worker and friend, I figured she would be more empathetic, which sent a much-needed wave of relief through me. However, upon seeing me, she scowled and immediately told me that she couldn't approve my application for food stamps, because she didn't think that I really needed the financial assistance. Stunned, I quickly rolled my baby out of her office, through the throngs of people waiting in line, and to the parking lot where I crumbled into fits of crying over my hopeless situation. When I finally replaced my defeat with determination, I turned to my in-laws, who, to my relief, were more than willing to offer financial support to my boys and me.

In retrospect, I realize that I could have opposed the ruling and, more than likely, my application would have been approved. But, my pride kept me from pursuing an avenue of government assistance even when I desperately needed it. I don't recommend allowing pride to govern common sense. When in need, government assistance can be a temporary solution until employment and finances are rectified.

For more information regarding food stamps and other federal and state assistance programs, call 1-800-221-5689 or visit the welfare information website at www.welfareinfo.org.

Smart Shopping

Due to my financial constraints and lack of food stamps, I turned to my college education in Home Economics, which helped me create strategies to stretch my household budget.

~Coupons

One of the greatest sources of coupons is your local Sunday newspaper. Clip and save only the coupons you think you will use. A simple filing system can be made with envelopes that are labeled and kept alphabetically; i.e., beverages, cereals, cleaning products, meats, medicines, produce, and toiletries. Make note of the coupons' expiration dates with a highlighter to keep your coupons current.

~Buy in Quantity

Generally, products packaged in large quantity are less expensive. If necessary, take a small calculator to the grocery store and calculate the cost per weight of products. Most grocery stores will post this information on their price label. Learn to read these labels; they state the exact cost per unit of an item.

When you buy a product in large quantity, you will need

to divide the product into smaller, usable amounts. If it is per-ishable, invest in freezer bags and place what you will not imme-diately use into the freezer for later use. Non-perishable items, such as detergent or powdered milk, can be placed in plastic containers.

~Discount Warehouses

Discount Warehouses often have damaged packages of food or appliances that are sold at a further discount, which can be as much as thirty to sixty percent off the original price. Call the warehouses in your area and ask if they sell such products.

All grocery stores have damaged goods sections where you will find an assortment of discounted items with reduced prices. Produce markets and roadside stands discount overly ripe bananas and other fruits and vegetables hoping to sell them quickly. Consider buying large quantities of discounted products that can be stored or frozen.

~Loss Leaders, In-store and Double Coupon Days

Loss leaders are items priced at the store's cost simply to attract more customers to the store. These items are generally a very good buy.

In-store coupons are found only in a specific store for a limited time. Often there are newspaper ads, inserts, or promo-tional flyers that are delivered to your home announcing in-store specials. Additional copies of these flyers are often posted near the front of the grocery store.

Many grocery stores offer double coupons on certain days, which offer twice the savings on a specified product.

Become familiar with the various marketing techniques used by the stores in your area and take advantage of the dis-counts to become a smart shopper. Coupons can reduce your grocery bill by as much as thirty-five percent. Be flexible when you shop and learn to buy what you need when it is on sale. Adjust your weekly menus accordingly and this flexibility will allow you to purchase more food at prices you can afford.

~Thrift Bread Stores

Thrift bread stores sell day-old and over-baked bread and pastries at approximately fifty percent off the regular grocery store price. About half of the breads available at thrift bread outlets are fresh products, and the remainder of the products on the shelves are probably day-old products that a supermarket has returned. Thrift stores keep breads on the shelves for only two days, so their discounted products are generally fresh enough for general consumption. Read the labels and the expiration dates on these products to ensure the best buys.

Buy bread in quantity and freeze it in plastic freezer bags, unthawing it as needed. Caution: storing bread in the refrigerator will cause it to become prematurely dry.

If your town does not have a thrift bread store, ask the manager at your local supermarket how you can obtain day-old bread products directly from his store. He most likely returns day-old products and may allow individuals to purchase these items before they are sent back to the bakery.

~Freezer Advantages

Invest in a freezer if possible; it can be the best food investment you make. Read the newspaper ads for a used freezer or check the Yellow Pages for a discount appliance center. Look for a freezer unit with a tight seal, cold interior, and no excess frost on the walls. When you find a freezer that appears to be in good condition and is within your budget, insist that the owners allow you to turn it on for twenty-four hours before you actually purchase it.

To test a freezer's working condition, place a bowl of

water in the center of the unit. If, after twenty-four hours, the water is not frozen solid or there is excess frost around the inside, the seal is probably broken. Seals are expensive to replace, so be particular about what you purchase.

A freezer allows you to cook and store large quantities of sauces, casseroles, bean and meat dishes, and other staples for future meals. Label and date each container placed in the freezer.

Stretching Your Clothing Budget

With the exception of socks and underwear, which should be purchased new, secondhand clothing can be found in every community at yard sales, used clothing shops and thrift stores.

When shopping for secondhand clothing, purchase clothes that you would choose if shopping at an ordinary retail store. Be willing to wait for the right thing. Do not buy items that are torn, missing buttons, zippers, or belts. Do not waste your time and money on clothing that needs excessive repair. Wash and iron secondhand clothing before you wear it. This will give it the appearance of being new. And, avoid clothing that needs dry cleaning. Dry cleaning costs can eat up the money you saved.

Take children eight years and older with you when you are shopping for secondhand clothing for them. And, allow teenagers to choose their own clothing; no clothing is a bargain if it is never worn.

Buy clothes off-season. For example, go to a yard sale and purchase a winter coat in July and a summer dress in November. Anticipate upcoming clothing needs like weddings or graduations, and begin shopping the used clothing stores well in advance of the event.

Dressing Teenagers on a Budget

Since most teens want to dress like their peers, you may

want to incorporate a clothing allowance for your teen to buy clothes at a popular retail store if the thrift stores don't meet all of their expectations.

Help teens compile two lists: need and want. Explain how much money they are allowed and help them to understand your financial limitations. Offer suggestions of how to best spend their clothing allowance and recommend that they ask sales consultants about upcoming sales events.

Help teens think through each purchase. Is it too faddish and will the article be quickly discarded? Can they see themselves wearing it next year? Do they have room to grow? Make every purchase count. You can teach your teenagers good shopping skills while keeping them within the family budget.

Shoes

Secondhand shoes that are fashionable and inexpensive may be located at secondhand clothing stores and thrift stores. Pay attention to comfort, style, and condition. Avoid shoes with worn heels or damage. The only thing you should think of replacing is the laces, so the other elements of the shoes should be in satisfactory condition. Once purchased, powder and vacuum used shoes and polish them to maintain their attractive appearance.

Secondhand Sports Equipment

Yard sales and used sporting goods stores are good sources for inexpensive sports and recreational equipment. Some schools help parents organize an equipment exchange in which everyone gathers on a chosen day to swap athletic shoes, various rackets, helmets, pads, gloves, balls, and the like. If your community does not have an event like this, inquire about beginning one. Some equipment swaps charge a one dollar entry fee to cover advertising costs.

Haircuts

An entire family can receive inexpensive haircuts at a local beauty school. Beauty school students usually offer permanents, hair coloring, manicures, facials, and other specialty treatments in addition to haircuts. You may want to request students who are nearing their graduation; however, there are always experienced supervisors on duty to help the students offer satisfactory service.

It is the wounded oyster that mends its shell with pearl.
—Ralph Waldo Emerson

12

Journaling

Journal Writing: A Road to Personal Recovery and Self-esteem

In the world of self-help, journaling has emerged as a useful form of personal exploration. A journal became the place where I transformed my sense of fragmentation into acceptance and learned to approach life empowered.

Simple writing exercises can guide you down a road to better emotional and physical health. Even if writing is difficult for you, there are exercises you can easily accomplish that will open your mind to what you are feeling, what you need, and what you want to change in your life. Journaling is not about good writing; rather, it is about communication. It is about recognizing and directing your life's path and choosing to walk towards recovery and self-esteem.

First, choose a notebook that will be used only for journaling and locate a private place to keep it in. This book is for you, about you, and there is no need to share its contents with anyone else unless it benefits you. However, it is important that you write in your journal with the certainty that it will never be read by anyone but you. Set aside a few minutes each day—first thing in the morning, just before bed, during lunch, or perhaps while you're doing the laundry. Make a commitment to write in your journal regularly.

You may approach the empty journal page with the feeling that you have nothing of importance to say. But, successful journal writing is about whatever is important to you at any given moment. Set aside your feelings of inadequacy as a writer. In your journal, you are an explorer in your world.

Warm-up Exercises
~Lists

Make lists in your journal of anything affecting your life; i.e., grievances, joys, pains, successes, heartache, doubts, fears, loves, and likes. Any list will do, but those that lead you into positive reflection will probably make you feel better about your life. However, lists of negative feelings are also helpful, because they allow you to acknowledge your emotions and disappointments.

~Letters

Write "imaginary" letters to people that have caused exceptional emotions in you, positive or negative. Detail the events that caused you to be affected by that person's actions, how you reacted to it, and how you feel about it presently. These letters may lend in resolving a problem.

~Stream of Consciousness Writing

Also called automatic writing, this exercise involves quickly writing whatever comes to your mind without first contemplating it. Don't worry about punctuation or spelling. Write without judgment. Try to write this way for three to five minutes, then close your notebook and go on about your day. You'll be surprised at how much you can release from your subconscious in this type of writing.

Journaling gave me the opportunity to look at my life story. You may find that a particular theme repeats in your entries, which may help you identify areas in your life to focus on. Explore your fears and thoughts in your notebook. You may discover topics that you want to discuss with a friend.

Journal writing is about recognizing yourself in your dramas and then guiding yourself into who you want to become. In your journal, you become conscious of your choices. And, as you become self-aware, you become better equipped to face the future with renewed confidence.

Journal Exercise For Those in a Family Arrested

The following questions directly address the problems and concerns of a prisoner's spouse.

• How did you feel about your spouse the day he left for prison?

• How did family, friends, co-workers, and the legal system treat you after your spouse's arrest?

• How has your life changed since your spouse left for prison?

• What new responsibilities do you have and how are you handling them?

• What are you doing for yourself to cope with this new lifestyle?

• What obstacles have you encountered?

• Which friends have been unsupportive?

• What keeps you going each day?

• Evaluate your behavior and attitude after each month since the incarceration. How are you adapting?

• When you speak with your spouse on the phone, do you feel better or worse? Why?

• How did you feel before, during, and after your first prison visit?

• How can you improve your communication with your spouse?

• How do you feel about the future?

These journal exercises encourage you to think about your "arrested" experience. It is not always a happy experience to write about. But, you want to move forward in your life, and journaling will allow you to see and record your progress. Remember: don't judge your answers as good or bad. You can only fail at journaling if you don't do it.

Prison Life

stage
III

To keep our faces toward change, and behave like free spirits in the presence of fate, is strength undefeatable.

—Helen Keller

13

Prison Life: Basic Guidelines

Most prisons will have an inmate's handbook describing the daily procedures for that particular institution. The inmate should become familiar with these guidelines.

Unit Team

In most prisons, each inmate will be assigned to a Unit Team upon arrival at the prison. A Unit Team is generally comprised of a Unit Manager, Case Manager, Counselor, and an Education Representative. A meeting with Unit Team members usually occurs within a month of the prisoner's arrival, and the date and time of the meeting is posted on the unit bulletin board; attendance is mandatory. The issues discussed at a team meeting may include:

- Length of sentence, court imposed fines, and court recommendations

• Educational, recreational, and counseling programs

• Eligibility for parole hearing and the time limit requirements for applying for the next appropriate docket

• Financial Responsibility Program/Restitution

• Status of detainer and outstanding charges

• Community Treatment Center or Halfway House (CTC) eligibility

• Issues presented by the inmate

• Documentation and completion of Visitor List

• Approximate date of next review

Program Review Team

Each inmate has a Program Review Team Meeting every ninety days. The purpose of these reviews usually includes:
• Discussion of programming progress

• Institutional adjustment

• Status of Financial Responsibility Program

• New information with reference to parole hearings and CTC eligibility

• Discussion of concerns initiated by inmate; i.e., transfer requests or detainer status

Other Unit Team involvement might consist of holding Unit Disciplinary Committee Hearings or visits to job sites. In most prisons, there may be a Unit Team available for individual consultation during non-scheduled team reviews. Some Case Managers may utilize an open door policy.

Phone Use

Phone usage rules vary by institution. The Unit Team will explain to the inmate:

- The process of signing up for phone use

- Unmonitored phone calls to an attorney

- Phone calls made by a Unit Staff in Counsel House Arrest or Case Manager Offices

Psychologists

Generally, there is a staff of psychologists available to the inmates. Mental health programs offered usually include psychological screening, crisis intervention, grief therapy, individual and group psychotherapy, psychological testing and evaluation, drug counseling, and suicide prevention.

Religion

Each institution varies in its religious activities, offerings, and schedule. Shortly after arrival, each inmate should receive a copy of the schedule of religious activities. The schedule will give the time, locale, and the person responsible for religious services, instruction, and devotions.

A chaplain should be assigned to each institution. Prisoner counseling is one of the most important roles handled by the prison chaplain. The chaplain will generally counsel inmates regarding all issues of importance to them.

Attendance at any religious service is voluntary. No inmate can be forced to attend, nor will he be kept from attending the religious service or activities of his choice.

Inmate Funds

At most institutions, if an inmate arrives with cash funds in his possession, he will be given a temporary receipt for those funds. Upon establishment of a commissary account, those funds are placed in his account. However, purchases usually cannot be made until a copy of the cashier's receipt has been received. The inmate usually receives cashier's receipts within two or three days after arrival. When the receipt is posted to the appropriate account, the inmate on the account may make purchases during the stipulated commissary sales hours.

To receive funds in prison, check with the policy requirements regarding which type of funds are acceptable. Some institutions require cashier's checks or money orders, which will generally be posted directly to an inmate's account. If the institution allows personal checks or company checks, they may be unavailable for a minimum of thirty days while they clear the bank. If an inmate wishes to send money to his family, he needs to see his Unit or Case Manager, who will arrange the appropriate forms. The Case Manager will deliver this form to the prison business office for processing. After funds have been deducted from the inmate's account, a copy of the form is routed to the inmate. In my experience, I received funds from my husband within two weeks via the U.S. postal system.

Commissary

The commissary is a shop inside the prison that offers merchandise for the prisoners to purchase. The amount an inmate is allowed to spend per month for regular commissary products will vary from year to year and institution to institution.

Special Purchase Orders (SPOs) are deducted from the monthly spending limitation. Generally, all items with a unit price in excess of twenty-five dollars are not deducted from the spending limit. In order to purchase a watch or other designated items, an inmate must first obtain clearance from the Receiving & Discharge (R&D) Officer or a designated staff member. The R&D Officer will issue a permit that allows the inmate to purchase certain items. Check with the Unit Counselor for a list of the items requiring such approval.

Coins

In some prisons inmates are allowed to buy coins or tokens, but the coins are sold by the roll only. Purchases of coin rolls usually do not count against each inmate's monthly spending limitation. However, in most prisons loose coins are not usually sold. Generally, the maximum coin amount an inmate is allowed to hold in his possession is twenty dollars. Coins in excess of this amount found on an inmate are considered contraband and will be confiscated by prison authorities.

Currently, the most sophisticated monetary system available in prisons is a name tag bar code which references purchases against an inmate's account. This system is usually found in institutions where traditional money is prohibited.

Stamps

Stamps are available for purchase on a weekly basis and generally don't count against the inmate's money allotment. Some institutions may provide stamps free of charge for mailing legal documents.

Photo Tickets

If a prison allows photographs to be taken, photo tickets are available for purchase at the commissary. Photo tickets are used as an exchange for the development of photos that have been taken in the prison during visitor hours.

Vending Machines
Vending machines are available for inmate use in some institutions. The vending machine companies do not provide refunds, nor is the prison responsible for any monetary losses that an inmate or visitor may incur.

Inmate mail
There are several rules that must be strictly followed in order to send letters, packages, or money orders to a prison.

~General prison postal rules:
When mailing a letter to the prison, the envelope must be addressed with the inmate's complete name, prison identification number, prison mail box number, and complete address of the prison. If the writing is not legible, the envelope may not be given to the inmate.

ADDRESSED ENVELOPE

Sender's Name	*correct*
Sender's Address	*postage*
Sender's City, State, Zip Code	
	Inmate's Name
	Inmate's ID #
	Prison Address/Inmate's Mailbox #
	City, State, Zip Code

~Letters and packages will NOT be delivered if they include:
• Cash

- Stamps
- Polaroid photographs
- Pornographic materials
- Unauthorized items (clothing, shoes, glasses, medicine, cigarettes, or food)
- Anything the correctional officer deems unacceptable

~Packages

Inmates may only receive packages containing magazines or books. Sending reading materials by "book rate" is generally less expensive. Magazines will be checked carefully, so don't try to slip something between the pages. Do not send pornographic materials; such actions can cause serious consequences. Some prisons only allow magazines and books that are shipped directly from a bookstore or publisher. Check the prison policies before shipping anything. The books must be wrapped, post-marked, and have the business address on the package or they will be returned.

~Authorization Forms

Packages containing certain items, such as clothing, shoes, eyeglasses, sunglasses, sports equipment, towels, and underwear will be accepted only if they contain an authorization form. It is my experience that the sender must follow the exact requirements on the authorization form. If the form identifies three pairs of white underwear, but three pairs of blue underwear are sent, the entire package may be returned to the sender. Do not change the number, color, or size of the items approved on the Package Authorization Form.

Everyone thinks of changing the world, but no one thinks of changing himself.

—Leo Tolstoy

14

Sentencing and Prison Records

The Prison Records Office

The major responsibilities of the Prison Records Office include the computation of the inmate's sentence, computation of Good Conduct Time (GCT), and the filing of a detainer—a writ for continuing to hold a person already in custody. If all of an inmate's documents are in order, the inmate should receive a copy of his sentence computation within thirty working days after his arrival at the prison. If an inmate's documents are not organized or complete, it may take longer to receive official records.

Sentence Computation:
• Date of sentencing

• Length of sentence

- Beginning date of sentence

- Jail Credits

- Date inmate was committed to the Federal or State Prison System

- Statutory Release Date

- Date sentence expires at its Full Term

- Rate per month and total amount of GCT

Good Conduct Time

The Comprehensive Crime Control Act of 1984 (CCCA) established a new form of "good time" credit for inmates sentenced under the CCCA provisions. The good time, which is referred to as GCT, is earned on sentences of one year and one day or more at a rate of fifty-four days for each year of time served, unless the Bureau of Prisons determines that the inmate has not satisfactorily complied with the institution disciplinary regulations. The statutory authority for GCT is contained in Title 18, U.S. Code, Section 3624 (b):

> "A prisoner who is serving a term of imprisonment of more than one year, other than a term of imprisonment for the duration of his life, shall receive credit toward the service of his sentence, beyond the time served, of fifty-four days a year of his term of imprisonment, beginning at the end of the first year of the term unless the Bureau of Prisons determines that, during that year, he has not satisfactorily complied with such institutional disciplinary regulations as have been

approved by the Attorney General and issued to the prisoner. If the Bureau determines that during that year the prisoner has not satisfactorily complied with such institutional regulations, he shall receive no such credit toward service of his sentence or shall receive such lesser credit as the Bureau determines to be appropriate. The Bureau's determination shall be made within fifteen days after the end of each year of the sentence. Such credit toward service of sentence vests at the time it is received."

Each state has its own statutes regarding GCT. This is subject to legislative change. You may want to request a copy of your state statutes and policies through your State Department of Corrections.

What lies behind us and what lies before us are tiny matters compared to what lies within us.

—Ralph Waldo Emerson

15

Inmate Health

Disclaimer: All information found in this chapter will probably vary from prison to prison. The following information provides general guidelines. Please check with each individual institution as to the exact policies.

Personal Hygiene Guidelines
Items provided by the prison:
• Soap
• Toothbrush/Toothpaste
• Comb
• Bathroom tissue
• Razor/Razor blades
• Shaving cream

Each inmate is expected to maintain a high standard of

personal hygiene, which includes a daily shower, a regular schedule of haircuts, and a daily change of clothing. Beards and mustaches are allowed, but facial hair must be covered when an inmate is working in Food Service or near machinery. Shaved heads, long hair, and afros are permitted if frequently groomed, but hair pieces are not allowed.

Each inmate is given a metal locker in which to keep his personal property. And, he is responsible for maintaining a high level of cleanliness and a sanitary environment in his dormitory, shower, toilet, washbasin, and recreation areas. Cleanliness ensures better health conditions and falls in line with prison fire prevention measures.

Standard Issue Clothing
- Underwear
- Socks
- T-shirts
- Work pants
- Work shirts

Generally, an inmate is also issued one pair of shoes or boots, one pair of cotton gloves, and if there is cold weather, a hat and a jacket. The inmate is responsible for the clothing. He must clean all the clothes, return all the clothes to the prison when leaving; and, if items are lost, the inmate must pay a fee to replace them.

Prison Health Services
~Physical Examinations
Common to new inmates, a physical exam will generally consist of a tetanus/diphtheria immunization, TB skin test, chest X-ray, eyesight screening, hearing test, dental exam, urinalysis, and blood tests. Generally, inmates fifty years of age and older

receive a medical exam every year, and inmates under fifty years receive a medical exam every two years.

When an inmate is transferred between prisons, a review of medical records replaces an exam. However, pre-release medical exams are usually offered to an inmate within the last sixty days of his sentence if the inmate has not had a complete physical exam within the past twelve months. Inmates interested in a pre-release medical exam should submit a written request to the prison's medical records office.

~General Outpatient Sick Call Procedure

All non-emergency medical care and pharmacy needs usually need to be obtained from a scheduled sick call appointment. Inmates desiring a sick call appointment usually report to the Health Services Center first thing in the morning. A physician's assistant or staff member issues appointment slips to the inmates, which are to be given to their supervisors upon reporting to work, or, if off work, to their dormitory officer. Inmates should report to the Health Services Center five minutes prior to their appointment with an institutional pass and their appointment slip.

~Procedure for Obtaining an Appointment with a Physician

The inmate needs to send a written request directly to the physician and then wait for written authorization. Special referral from sick call is generally made by the physician's assistant.

~Procedure for Obtaining Dental Appointments

Emergency dental appointments may be requested from the physician's assistant. Depending on the institution's policies, an emergency appointment will be issued immediately. Non-emergency dental appointments are usually obtained by sending a written request to the dentist.

~Pharmacy Services

Prescriptions must be written by the prison's physician or dentist. If an inmate is required to consume the medicine under supervision, a physician's assistant or a registered nurse will be present to document the consumption. If several doses of pre-scribed medicine are missed, the inmate's prescription will usual-ly be canceled. To have a prescription refilled, place a request for a sick call appointment.

~Surgery

At most prisons, the physician or physician's assistant performs minor procedures. These include excision of warts, moles, sebaceous cysts, ingrown toenails, and suturing lacera-tions. Elective major medical surgical procedures for inmates in federal prison are generally referred to a Bureau of Prisons (BOP) medical referral center if the patient is willing to transfer. At most prisons, emergency referrals go to the nearest local hos-pital.

~Emergency Appointments

Emergency Appointments (any appointment necessary and not obtained during a scheduled appointment time) are usu-ally available for sudden injuries. At most prisons, emergency appointments are not available for minor ailments, such as the common cold, nor are they available for injuries that weren't reported immediately.

~Medical Care in Solitary Confinement

Inmates housed in administrative detention or discipli-nary segregation, otherwise known as "the hole" or "solitary confinement," are also given the opportunity to present their medical/dental problems to medical personnel. At most prisons, a physician's assistant visits each inmate in isolation every morning, including weekends and holidays. At this time, inmates should report their medical/dental problems to the physician's assistant. In addition, a physician's assistant visits inmates daily to dispense prescribed medicine.

~Medically Prescribed Diets

At most prisons, inmates who require medically pre-scribed diets must be able to select the appropriate food items from the main menu. Specially prepared items are generally not available. Anyone requiring specially prepared food for a med-ically prescribed diet may be transferred to an institution that is equipped to handle such requests.

~Specialty Clinics

Inmates with chronic medical problems are usually evaluated by a physician at least once a month at a specialty clin-ic within the prison grounds. Inmates reporting to a specialty clinic are commonly asked to bring their prescribed medicine with them.

~Miscellaneous Health Issues

Prescription eyeglasses or contact lenses and orthopedic items may be mailed to the inmate's counselor or other designat-ed recipients for issuance to the inmate only after permission is granted. Non-prescription sunglasses, medicine, vitamins, and medical supplies may not be mailed to the inmate.

Drug Testing

Every inmate will be tested repeatedly for drugs and alco-hol use. An inmate will usually be tested during his admittance to prison, tested randomly throughout his sentence, and tested after returning from a furlough.

Although there isn't a national standard for prison drug testing, there are certain guidelines and types of tests followed by the lab that conducts drug testing for the prisons. Moreover, with the increase of technoligical advances, types of drug testing are constantly changing and improving.

~Chain of Custody

Every specimen must have a Chain of Custody form attached to it, as it is the most important aspect of a drug test. This form is kept with the specimen at all times and includes a statement signed by the inmate stating that he acknowledges the drug testing. If, at any time, the specimen is moved, handled, tested, or used in any way, the action must be recorded on the Chain of Custody form.

~Emit Method

The Emit Method of testing a urine sample identifies up to ten different drugs within twenty minutes. The technician may ask the inmate which drugs (over the counter or prescription) have been placed in his system in the last seven days.

If an inmate fails to produce urine for a drug test, the test is classified as "dirty" or positive test, meaning drugs appeared in the Urine Analysis (UA). If the inmate is simply dehydrated and can't produce a sample, the test is classified as False/Positive. Since a percentage of all UA tests will be False/Positive, a second test is given.

After producing a specimen, the inmate will need to sign a Legal Evidence Tape, which will be placed across the top of the bottle. The Legal Evidence Tape is very fragile; any tampering with the bottle will tear the tape and void the sample.

At most prisons, a positive test sample is kept for up to one year. It is frozen to prevent bacterial growth; and, if there is any possibility of legal action concerning a sample, the lab will keep the sample frozen indefinitely.

~GCMS Test

The Gas Chromatography Mass Spectrometer test (GCMS) is a thirty minute ion test that can identify virtually every kind of drug, but looks specifically for the drug that showed up in the first emit test. The GCMS instrument measures the exact quantity of drug in the urine. Drugs can also be detected in the liver, blood, and even in hair.

~Hair Analysis

Hair Analysis utilizes the entire strand of hair to impart the entire drug history of an individual. The usefulness and fallibility of this test is directly related to the length of the individual's hair and how quickly it grows. For example, if an inmate's head is shaved, his entire drug history will be instantly eliminated; hence, new hair growth will only reveal drug use relevant to the time frame of the new growth.

~False/Positive Test: An Inmate's Rights

Even with the sophistication of today's drug tests, mistakes, such as False/Positive, which claims an inmate has illegal drugs in his system when he doesn't, occur because of human error. A positive drug test will generally result in the inmate being placed in "the hole" for a few weeks, losing his earned good time. Upon release from prison, he will be consistently drug tested while on parole.

If an inmate tests positive, but has not used drugs, he may be unable to defend himself. It could be necessary for the family to become involved. Therefore, it is wise for an inmate and his family to know the various tests, the meaning of each step, results of the tests, and what an inmate's rights are throughout the drug testing procedure.

The best defense against a False/Positive is to make the inmate aware of the importance of each step of the specimen's labeling, especially the Legal Evidence Tape. Yet, in the event of a False/Positive, call a lawyer. Legal counsel is well worth the expense you may incur clearing an inmate's record. If you are able to pay the testing fee, request a new drug test for the inmate, as you may be able to challenge the results of the False/Positive drug test. Depending on the institution, the inmate may have to pay for the new test, but if it comes back negative, the institute might reimburse the inmate and clear his record.

Also, in the event of a False/Positive ask to see a copy of the Chain of Custody. Ask if there was a Legal Evidence Tape used and if it is attached to the specimen.

~Testing After Furloughs

Inmates of most institutions returning from a furlough or day pass will probably be tested for drugs. However, any type of drug testing performed outside of the prison at the inmate's discretion will not be considered valid by the prison officials.

A gem is not polished without rubbing, nor a man perfected without trials.

—Chinese Proverb

16

Emergencies and Furloughs

Emergencies

A correctional officer's supervisor is often the person to decide if the institution will call an inmate's family regarding an emergency; however, there are no rules requiring such notification. Therefore, in order to avoid undue worry for family members, I recommend that every inmate and his family set up an emergency communication system between the prison and home.

I had come to expect daily phone calls from my husband while he was in prison; however, at one point, several days passed without a phone call and I became worried. When I finally received a call from him, he explained that drugs had been found in his room, which prompted administrative detention for him and his three roommates. Although he was eventually cleared and released from "the hole," I was a nervous wreck until communication was re-established. After that experience, I realized if my husband couldn't call me, I had no way of remaining updated on his status. Therefore, I created an emergency communication system.

Emergency Communication System

An Emergency Communication System begins with your incarcerated loved one delegating a trustworthy fellow prisoner, preferably not a cellmate, to serve as a contact for your family in the event of an emergency. This person should be given your home phone number and at least one other phone number of a family member or friend. Then, if your loved one is placed in the hole and is left without access to a phone, your family will be contacted by the delegated person. Bear in mind, this system should be periodically updated since prison populations frequently change.

Family Emergencies "On the Outside"

Whether or not an emergency pass is issued to an inmate depends upon the crime committed by the inmate and the severity of the family member's emergency. Unless the inmate's crime is non-drug related and he has less than two years to serve, there is a very slim chance that the prison will issue an emergency furlough.

Emergency Passes

If an emergency pass is granted, be prepared to pay for all the expenses. If the inmate is in a high security level facility, he will probably have to travel in shackles and chains, while escorted by a corrections officer. So, bear in mind that the fee incurred by an escorted furlough will be charged to the inmate's family. Moreover, the inmate will have to spend the night at the county jail or the nearest prison facility. Many inmates turn down an emergency furlough when they learn of the restrictions. Be sure you are aware of all the implications of an emergency furlough before you accept it.

To obtain an emergency pass, call the warden. If he is not available, speak with the assistant, the inmate's counselor, or the chaplain. You may want to contact your lawyer, as lawyers are usually familiar with a prison's rules and regulations regarding emergency passes, which may save you hours of frustration. If possible, obtain the prison's policies regarding emergency passes before there is an actual emergency. Each institution will handle family emergencies differently. Write down the prison's procedures and keep this with your Home Emergency Chart.

Do not expect that an emergency pass will be granted. Even in the case of serious illness and even death, emergency passes are often refused.

However, when an emergency pass is granted, the inmate will probably need to sign a Conditions of Furlough form, which explains the details and restrictions of the pass. Remember, every rule and guideline must be followed exactly; a troublesome furlough could add time to the inmate's prison sentence.

Legal Furloughs

Occasionally, an inmate may be granted a legal furlough. Issues of a legal nature, such as IRS complications or bankruptcy hearings, would constitute grounds for a legal furlough. Contact your lawyer for more information about Legal Furloughs.

Transfer Furloughs

When an inmate is en route to a halfway house, he travels on a transfer furlough. He must follow all the guidelines stated in the furlough document and is still under the jurisdiction of the prison.

Social Furloughs

Institutions may have a policy regarding social furloughs; however, they are potentially risky for the warden. If the inmate, while on a furlough, causes even the slightest bit of trouble, the warden exposes himself to unwanted negative publicity. Because of that risk, most wardens are very restrictive about approving social furloughs, and, consequently, most institutions have eliminated them.

Home Emergency Chart

* * *

Correctional Facility:

Phone Number:

Address:

City, County, State, Zip:

Warden's Name

_____ Ext. _____

Assistant Warden

_____ Ext. _____

Chaplain's Name

_____ Ext. _____

Inmate's Job Area

_____ Ext. _____

Employer's Name

_____ Ext. _____

Counselor's Name

_____ Ext. _____

Lawyer's Name /Phone

_____

Lawyer's Address

_____

Inmate Emergency Chart

* * *

Inmate's Designated Contacts: (Update every six months)

1.

2.

3.

4.

5.

6.

In case of an emergency please call:

Name/Phone   Relationship

_____   _____

_____

_____   _____

_____

_____   _____

_____

Inmate Medical History

* * *

_____

_____

_____

_____

_____

_____

_____

_____

Reference:

Physician's Name:

Physician's Phone Number:

Other Information:

The Aftermath

stage

IV

In the battle between the stream and the stone, the stream always wins.....not through strength, but through persistence.

—Anonymous

17

Coming Home

I do not want to take away the joy and anticipation of the homecoming of your spouse; but, make no mistake about it, the homecoming is tough. There isn't an official welcome home ceremony for the returning inmate as there is for a soldier returning from war. By contrast, most wives and children of an inmate do not want to call public attention to their loved one's release from prison. The family has endured enough pain and humiliation from the impact of their loved one's arrest and subsequent prison sentence. Moreover, the daily challenges will continue even after the inmate has returned to the family home.

Marriage
Prison Fellowship has revealed that eighty percent of marriages fail after a spouse goes to prison. I have interviewed couples that have survived the homecoming and couples that have separated afterwards. But, once the inmate returns home,

you are again facing unknown circumstances. Over the time that passed without your spouse, you have probably become a very independent person, perhaps quite different from the person you were before your loved one's incarceration began. Your spouse has changed too; he has lived a life you can hardly imagine. Therefore, the first step towards rebuilding your marriage is accepting the fact that things will not be the same as before your spouse's incarceration.

Our "Practice Homecoming"

Our family was given the opportunity to have a "practice homecoming" two and a half years into my husband's fifteen year prison sentence. My husband was given an emergency four day furlough when his father became critically ill. We all learned much from the experience, and it foretold the tensions and stresses that would be inherent in the permanent homecoming that was still many years away.

During the four day furlough, my husband's arrest and incarceration seemed to fade from our family's memory. Everyone placed their pain into mental storage and leapt into the homecoming with vigor. The children and I were excited to share our daily lives with my husband; so, we drove him around the neighborhood, and visited stores, schools, and playgrounds that we frequented. I cooked special meals to celebrate his days with us. The children shared pictures of the last few years, favorite posters, books, and other things to bring their father current with their lives. This short visit reinforced my belief that once a loved one's incarceration is over, prison and all of its unpleasant details are blocked as much as possible from the family's collective memory. It is therefore necessary, as explained in previous chapters, that during an inmate's prison term his family continue to experience life on the outside as "normally" as possible. It is the good times that you will remember. Give your children a positive and happy childhood to carry forth with them. Their father's incarceration will be an agonizing chapter they will want to place behind them.

The four day furlough also introduced my family and me to the more difficult aspects of an inmate's homecoming. The first night my husband was home I prepared a turkey dinner, which was a treat for everyone. But, when dinner ended my sons left the table with their father, leaving me to clean up the table and kitchen alone. I had spent the past two and a half years teaching my sons to clear and wipe the dinner table, sweep the floor, put away leftovers, and wash the dishes with me. Yet, on the first night of their father's return, the mealtime pattern I had worked so hard to instill in the boys had vanished.

At the time, I believed my anger was about my husband's insensitivity to the shared mealtime chores. I stood by the table remembering all the nights the boys and I had cleaned up dinner together without my husband and was furious with my husband's disruption of our mealtime pattern. I was also angry that my husband expected me to serve him and clean up without any help. I had expected to be treated better. However, my irritation was really about more than the dinner mess. That one incident brought up the anger I had accumulated and carried within me since the day my husband was imprisoned. I did not know or see it at the time, but my fury was really about my husband's incarceration, which left me alone with the children and the responsibilities of our home. At that time, I had never spoken about those feelings, and my husband had no idea that he had done anything wrong. He was following a pattern of behavior consistent with our home life prior to his incarceration and was unaware of the changes in our mealtime routine. Essentially, being abandoned in the kitchen with a sink full of dirty dishes triggered unresolved feelings I was harboring towards my husband. Therefore, I recommend sharing all feelings between spouses if the marriage is to survive the homecoming of the inmate.

The problems experienced in a marital relationship before incarceration will not be magically erased during the years of a spouse's imprisonment. In fact, those same problems may have become more defined with the passing of time. If communication was difficult before incarceration, it will probably be even more so afterwards. Positive changes will come only through effective communication and understanding. This takes time and a willingness to be patient with one another.

Remember, the inmate has dreamed of his homecoming for years. He may have pictured a perfect home with perfect relationships among his wife and family. But the reality may be completely opposite from his dream of coming home, and he may experience great disappointment, even shock, when he is confronted by the reality of his home and family. Similarly, a wife may have imagined her husband has become the ideal mate during his absence, only to find that all of his former shortcomings still exist, which may be more pronounced upon his return from prison.

The former inmate must understand that time has passed and things may not be as they used to be. He may have clung to memories of how life was before incarceration, but upon returning home, he must look at life around him as something completely new.

Inmate Survival Mode Behavior

Living in prison bears no resemblance to home and family life. And, there is little or no trust between inmates, which propagates a survival mode form of behavior—addressing only the needs of self. Therefore, the returning inmate often cannot shed this mode of existence the moment he departs the prison gates, leaving the family to contend with a person who brings cynicism and self-centeredness to the family dynamic.

Cynical and negative attitudes are common to inmate mentality. Not only do prisoners experience a shift in attitude throughout their prison sentence, but the prison staff is also affected by the negativity of the environment. For instance, a former co-worker of mine left the youth ministry to accept a position as a corrections officer for a prison; and, even though I warned him of the bleak atmosphere and the possible side effects it could have on his personal life, he continued working for the prison. However, within two years, his personality shifted from one of compassion and lightheartedness to one of negativity. Subsequently, his once thriving marriage began to suffer and ultimately ended in divorce, with his wife commenting on his negative attitude as a basis for their unresolved problems.

Unfortunately, the survival mode behavior developed in prison usually continues on the outside for some time. The inmate's family is going to be subject to survival mode habits. The ex-prisoner may view the world in a cold-hearted, simplistic manner, looking for the bad elements in a person or situation as his initial instinct. And, there is the possibility that he may have developed a personality based on self-serving cynicism that will permeate the rest of his life. Hopefuly, with time and support from a loving family, the inmate will eventually recognize the positive in life and rediscover who he was prior to prison life.

Homecoming Issues for the Wife

While your loved one was away in prison, you learned to cope alone with the ups and downs of daily living. You learned to make decisions about money, housing, jobs, and schools, and you formed habits, schedules, and daily routines that you became comfortable with. The house is organized in a way that pleases you. In short, you have put your life in order without a husband.

When your husband returns home, he will need a sense

of space for himself. He may listen to a certain radio station, want his coffee made a certain way, and have different food preferences than the family. Every aspect of the family's daily routine may come under scrutiny and criticism, and you must decide how much of your independence you are willing to part with.

Even a returning spouse's efforts to be helpful can be viewed as inconsiderate by his family. After my husband returned from prison, he decided to have a garage sale in order to organize and pare down his old belongings. He chose to do this on a weekend I was scheduled to be out of town. Before I left I added some of my things to the sale pile, but told him not to sell anything else of mine. However, when I came home while the sale was in progress, I immediately spotted a table of sale items that not only included my favorite cake plate, which had been given to me by my great-aunt, but also my cherished backgammon board that I had brought home from Syria years before. Needless to say, I was furious. I had saved all of my husband's belongings for the six years he was incarcerated. Yet, in my two day absence, he randomly went through my personal items for his garage sale. He thought he was being helpful; it never occurred to him that he was invading my privacy. At that moment, I could see that we had a very serious communication problem—he was making family decisions without consulting me.

Communication may not come naturally to the returning spouse; therefore, you should expect this behavior and learn to gently, but firmly, remind your spouse that the survival mode behavior that was useful in prison is not welcome at home.

Marital Decisions

Your marriage will probably be in need of repair. Yet, if you have remained together, you have done so in spite of tremendous odds against you. Marital counseling is extremely helpful to a couple during this time of transition.

Questions which help analyze your marriage:

• Should you remain married?

• Has your life become too independent from his to share a home and partnership?

• Does your husband treat you in an abusive manner?

• Does your husband accept your new lifestyle?

• Can you accept any changes in his character?

• Is there a common ground of love from which to move forward?

• What is his vision of the future?

• What is your vision of the future?

The Return of Your Sex Partner

Unfortunately, there are a large number of inmates that contract Sexually Transmitted Diseases (STDs) in prison. Ask your spouse to be tested for STDs before you engage in sexual activity. According to a new statistic, the fastest growing population of hepatitis C cases are black women, and of these women, the majority of them are contracting hepatitis C from their husbands and boyfriends that have served time in prison.

Children, Discipline, and the Returning Inmate

If you have children living at home, expect conflicting opinions between you and your returned spouse concerning discipline, family rules, and guidelines. Your spouse may want to step in and take over. He may be very strict with the children, or he may become more interested in regaining their trust and try to be a friend to them instead of a parent. Either way, you are going to feel frustrated until a balanced parenting plan is established.

The more you can share about your parenting choices with your spouse, the smoother his transition from absent parent to active parent will be. The former inmate needs to understand that he cannot step into the family home and assume total control over the children's lives. He must see that the family has been a functioning unit without him and that the members of the family are not going to abandon their established lifestyles.

If you have teenagers, there will be added tensions. Dating, curfew, car privileges, friends, school work, and clothing preferences can be the source of parent-child friction. Before the returning father can expect to exert any authority over his teenager, he must first reconcile his relationship with them. The response to the returning parent can be very different among children of different ages. When a former inmate and friend of mine returned home to his two pre-school children and one high school daughter, he found the younger children adapted very well to his homecoming, but the teenager, in an attempt to get her own way, used her father's return to drive a wedge between her parents. When she could not obtain permission from her mother, she went to her father. When permission could not be obtained from either, she focused her anger on her father, reminding her mother of the embarrassment and trouble he had caused the family, rejecting him completely and blaming him for ruining her life. In this way, she caused friction in the family. Only after the husband and wife established a concrete plan of discipline for their teenager did their family life begin to calm down.

Give It Time

A former inmate's re-entry into society and into the family must be given first priority. Some inmates arrive home anxious to make up for lost time and literally wear their families out, emotionally and physically, smothering their loved ones with attention, advice, opinions, and criticism. This sort of frenzied re-entry can result in misunderstandings and create a sort of push-pull relationship. Remember, like all of the passages undergone in the years of a loved one's incarceration, homecoming takes time. Readjustment to one another is a process that must be allowed to unfold slowly.

The Halfway House

Many inmates find that after years of being separated from their families, they need to re-enter their family's life in small steps. The halfway house provides a gradual re-entry method for many inmates and their families. In terms of adjusting to life outside of prison, a halfway house is a place that is halfway between prison and home. As a continuation of the prison sentence, almost all prisoners are released from prison into a halfway house. About a month before an inmate is to leave for a halfway house, he should get a complete list of required paperwork from the prison. At that time, the prisoner should begin contacting employers and friends to initiate his job search. He must hold a current driver's license, proof of insurance, and a car before he can be released to a higher privilege level at the halfway house. Thorough planning prior to release can save the prisoner and his family hours of frustration later on.

Most prisons will place an inmate into the halfway house closest to his family or closest to the location of his original legal proceedings. An inmate must sleep at the halfway house, but he is gradually given more privileges as he earns them. However, an inmate is generally given a weekend furlough before his time at the halfway house is completed.

An inmate at a halfway house must follow very strict rules, just as in prison. There are frequent urine analysis tests, and the violation of any rule, especially those related to drug and alcohol use, is a forfeiture of all good time and a rapid return to prison. For some prisoners, the freedoms of a halfway house are too difficult to handle, and many inmates choose to complete their full prison sentence by staying in prison rather than risk breaking a rule at a halfway house.

However, a halfway house offers an inmate the opportunity to re-enter society in small steps. Although finding a job is usually difficult, an inmate has the opportunity to begin working within society again, which helps him rebuild his self-esteem and also earn money for his family. Part of an inmate's salary, often twenty-five percent, goes directly to the halfway house where he is staying.

Most halfway house inmates accept any job they can find, since holding a job enables an inmate to earn higher privilege levels. The higher the privilege level, the more liberal the restrictions are for an inmate. As an inmate becomes more trusted at the halfway house and at his job, his curfew may be extended and he will probably be given weekend furloughs with his family. Bear in mind that some states hold policies requiring the released inmate to secure a job within two weeks or he will have to return to prison.

When relegated time in the halfway house is over, an inmate will either be fully released from prison or he will be ordered to serve Home Confinement.

Home Confinement
The Bureau of Prisons may allow Home Confinement,

which allows an inmate to go home before his "official time" is up. Often this is done when there is overcrowding at a halfway house and space is needed for inmates who require more supervision. When an inmate is given Home Confinement, the Bureau of Prisons has deemed him a good risk and will allow him to finish his sentence at home, provided he follows certain rules. Individual states may or may not offer Home Confinement. Check with your state's Department of Corrections regarding policies.

Typically, an inmate under the regulations of Home Confinement must be home by 8:00 PM each evening and not leave the house before 6:00 AM. The inmate must be home and available to talk with a parole officer at any hour of the night. And, the inmate and his family must be willing to have their home searched by a parole officer during any of the hours that the inmate is required to be at home. Part of a parole officer's visit may include a drug/alcohol test. Therefore, the family of the inmate must assume that the parole officer will visit their home unexpectedly once a week or every day, including New Year's Eve, Christmas, a family birthday, or weekends.

Remember: the parole officer will visit the inmate's home as often as he believes is necessary to assure the parole board that the inmate is following Home Confinement rules. *Any* infraction of *any* rule will mean loss of all the inmate's good time and his immediate return to prison.

Community Service Programs

Several state institutions have developed community service programs to replace the halfway house system. Day center programs provide treatment for drug and alcohol abuse, academic classes, and computer courses in order to encourage the rehibilitation of inmates re-entering society.

Federal Bonding Program

It often is hard for a convicted felon to obtain a job that requires bonding. The Federal Bonding Program (FBP) was developed by the U.S. Department of Labor in 1966 to help high risk groups of potential employees qualify for fidelity insurance coverage. Fidelity bonding is insurance that protects employers against employee theft or dishonesty. FBP coverage is provided at no cost to the employer or the job applicant if the applicant finds he is not commercially bondable and has a firm job offer or is qualified for the job. The job must offer full-time employment; however, self-employment is not applicable.

The job applicant or the prospective employer may apply for FBP insurance at any local State Employment Security Agency, State Job Service, or State Employment Service. For more information about the Federal Bonding Program, call (800) 233-2258.

Life is no brief candle to me. It is a sort of splendid torch, which I have got a hold of for the moment, and I want to make it burn as brightly as possible before handing it on to future generations.
—George Bernard Shaw

18

My Life Since the Arrest

As I write this last chapter, it has been almost sixteen years since my husband was arrested. My life has taken some paths and directions that I would never have anticipated nor desired. However, even after everything that has fallen on my shoulders, I feel blessed. Therefore, this last chapter offers hope by sharing some of the insights that I have discovered through my own personal experiences about incarceration and its impact on family members.

The day my husband left for prison I was financially broke, I just did not know it. And, over time my situation worsened. My youngest son had a medical condition called "failure to thrive," and at one year he weighed only eight pounds. He was supported by oxygen for two years, and the doctors feared that if he contracted an illness as simple as a common cold, it could quickly compound into pneumonia and he would die. Therefore,

I could not pursue traditional jobs; I needed to stay home with my baby and keep him away from all possible health dangers.

Another area of the stressful lifestyle that was imposed upon me was my relationship with the IRS. Part of the plea agreement that my husband signed included a charge by the IRS. At the time of the plea agreement, we thought the charge was insignificant, because we knew we didn't owe the IRS money. And, after all, the IRS charge was to run concurrently with the prison sentence. So, we didn't consider it a looming problem.

However, the IRS forced me to participate in a hearing where I represented myself Pro Se, since I had no money to pay attorneys. They told me they would "take every penny I earned over thirty thousand dollars per year." Therefore, I could not earn enough money to hire someone to take care of my baby in our home. Moreover, placing him in a daycare facility was out of the question on account of his fragile health.

During the first few years, I met with eighteen IRS agents. No one could, or would, settle my case. The IRS fees and charges against my family escalated to over $3.5 million over several years while my husband was in prison, leaving me in fear of the IRS for years to follow. Initially, the IRS seized our checking and saving accounts; so, for more than ten years I was frightened to open a checking account in my name. After the boys got older and my baby's health stabilized, I tried to get a job that paid a decent salary. Yet, when the employment agency discovered that I did not have a bank account, and with further research discovered the IRS lien, the agency never returned my phone calls. But with persistence and faith in God, I discovered jobs, friends, and mentors that opened doors to me.

Finding a Faith Community
After my husband was indicted, his story appeared on TV and in the newspapers for several weeks, which alerted the

community and people in my spiritual circle to my predicament; however, no one, including the pastor and congregation of the church I attended, contacted me to offer support. Yet, I knew that with my husband in prison, the boys and I needed to be involved in a faith community.

Upon the reference of a good friend, I was directed to The Rev. Dr. David Poling. He was kind and welcomed my husband and me into his church. Not only did he make us feel comfortable, but he accepted us unconditionally and prayed for us. We decided immediately to join Dr. Poling's congregation. However, part of the "welcoming" to his church was the introduction of new members to the governing members of the church council. What should have been considered a lovely event sent me into a panic attack, causing me to consider backing out. In fact, a member of Dr. Poling's governing board had been a former banker of ours that had called in all of our bank loans, and I was convinced that if he had anything to say about us joining "his church" that we would be blackballed and not allowed to join. But, I forced myself to attend the introduction of new members, and when I saw our banker, I stayed clear of him. In spite of my fears, I met several kind people and my family was accepted as new members of the church. I cannot remember a time in my life when I was so relieved to be accepted into a group.

Do not think you are alone if you, too, have worried about joining a faith community. Please take my advice: meet with the head of staff first. Make sure you have his/her blessing before joining a congregation. Furthermore, join a congregation that is happy to have you and rejoices because you are there.

Once I was accepted into the new church, I wanted to get to know the members. Once a week my boys attended a children's program and I worked as a volunteer on various committees. Several months later an associate pastor asked me to travel to San Diego to attend a Leadership Training School that was offered by LOGOS System Associates. After much internal debate with myself, I finally agreed to attend the training. Of course, my fantasies of relaxing at the beach, eating in fancy restaurants, and shopping never materialized. Instead, my mind became filled with the most exciting information I had ever heard. I learned how members in a church could truly become "church family" through the relationships that were formed in the LOGOS Program.

LOGOS, a midweek program for youth and children, is utilized in urban, rural, and suburban churches, representing over twenty-six denominations in the United States, Canada, Japan, Russia, and other countries. LOGOS' structure is comprised of four components—bible study, singing, play time, and meal time—which foster meaningful Christian relationships. I felt completely blessed to attend a LOGOS School where Dr. Dale K. Milligan, Founder and Executive Director of LOGOS, was leading the school. I absorbed every word he spoke for three days, and when I returned home from San Diego I realized that I had eaten out at one restaurant, viewed the beach from the airplane, and had never even thought about shopping. However, I was filled with an energy and new sense of direction that I believe came from the Holy Spirit.

Two church staff members had accompanied me to the training school, and since the LOGOS Program recommends that a Lay Leader be in charge of the program, I was chosen to be Director of our church's LOGOS Program. The form that LOGOS suggested its leaders sign encouraged prayer and discernment regarding acceptance of the new leadership position. I had never prayed about a leadership position in my life. Leadership came very easy to me, so I never even thought about it. But, with LOGOS, I was asked to pray about this position. For the first time in my life, I was promising God that I would try to do my best. I prayed for a week about the decision to become the first LOGOS Director at our church. Finally, I felt that I was divinely "called" to this position and accepted it. I embraced the position with all of my heart. I loved the way I was being supported and nurtured, and the boys were also blessed having so many adults and other children in their lives.

The following year, we had more than two hundred youth and children in the program, so the church leadership decided they needed to hire a Youth Director.

Youth Director

Dr. Poling, the Senior Pastor who had welcomed my family into his church, had the courage to ask me to fill the role of Youth Director. Again I prayed about accepting a new position. *Could I do the job? Who was I, the wife of a prisoner, to be leading others to Christ?* My doubts humbled me; however, I felt that the year I served as volunteer LOGOS Director had prepared me for the new position.

I embraced the job and enjoyed working with the youth. I loved the challenge of creating ways to get the youth involved in local and global mission work. To help cultivate the youth program, my colleagues and I decided to organize a foreign mission trip. The national Presbyterian Church assigned us to create a Vacation Bible School for four churches on the Island of Grand Cayman. Sixteen youth and four adults participated in that mission trip. When I was asked to teach a class about Christ, I was suddenly faced with the task of understanding my own faith. But, along with the missionary group, I taught hundreds of Cayman children and youth about Christ. We knew we were making a difference when we would drive by the beaches in the afternoons and see children out in the water teaching their friends the motions to one of our favorite songs, "Pharaoh, Pharaoh!"

I remained Youth Director at the church for five years, and in 1988 I accepted a position on the National LOGOS Board. I became acquainted with caring pastors and lay leaders from churches around the country. As a National LOGOS Board member, I quickly took on the responsibilities of a presenter for LOGOS' training seminars around the country. I relied on my college education, flight attendant training, and hotel management skills to help coordinate national meetings in hotels and retreat centers. One of my larger tasks was to organize a mission trip to Russia for the summer of 1993.

In March of 1993, I learned that my husband was going to be released in August after serving six years of his fifteen year sentence. I walked into the church staff meeting that morning delighted and anxious to share my good news. Within minutes of taking my place, I blurted out the news of my husband being released from prison in five months. Unfortunately, Dr. Poling had changed pastorates by then. The new Senior Pastor responded to my announcement by saying, "I can no longer be your pastor." I was stunned! I thought I misunderstood him. Yet, I looked across the room and our female pastor, Rev. K., had burst into tears before leaving the room. Suddenly the tears flowed down my cheeks at the thought of the pastor's harsh words, and I left the room to commiserate with Rev. K. I was in shock. How could I work in a church where *the* pastor could not be *my* pastor? I was devastated. Yet, I decided to stay for the next five months, as we had five youth from our church that were part of the first LOGOS Team to Russia, and I wanted the rest of the youth to experience what had been planned for that summer.

I quit working at the church three days after my husband came home from prison. It was very difficult saying goodbye to all the youth and staff; nevertheless, I could not stay at a church where the pastor refused to be a pastor to me.

LOGOS in Russia

In December of 1990, LOGOS was invited to Russia for the first time. Four representatives from LOGOS made the first trip to Russia. There they met Vassily Telitcyn, a sixty-nine-year-old retired accountant, who was from the Russian Far East, which was eight time zones from Moscow. After learning of LOGOS, he had pleaded, "Please bring us something for our children." Hence, in the summer of 1993, thirty-nine Americans, including Dr. Dale K. Milligan, were involved in LOGOS' first youth trip to Russia. Rev. Randy Webb led the team and I was his assistant, traveling from one end of Russia to the other. We traveled to Moscow, St. Petersburg, Irkutsk, Siberia, Khabarovsk, Chegdomyn in the Russian Far East, Anchorage, and home to our final destination cities. Five youth from our church, including my oldest son, were part of this team. I felt "called" upon and prepared to help lead this trip. However, one of the primary reasons for going on the trip was to be with my son. I wanted him to share his faith with others, while experiencing some of the joy that came from mission work.

LOGOS in Reform Schools

I have encountered ten mission trips to Russia since 1993. Yet, noteworthy is one of the first trips, in which I visited a Boys' Reform School in Irkutsk, Siberia. It was a dreary place, surrounded by barbed wire, high walls, and an intimidating entrance. The boys all appeared to be in their early teens. Due to malnourishment, they were thin, and their heads were shaved to manage lice infestations. The corrections officers, as well as the boys, were unwelcoming; nevertheless, we proceeded to visit with the youth, play games, and distribute socks, shampoo, soap, toothpaste, toothbrushes, and Latin crosses that had been cross-stitched by an American church group.

Upon our next visit to the boys' reform school, we saw

the front window filled with boys who were proudly holding their Latin crosses next to their faces. The boys, as well as the corrections officers, greeted us with hugs and flowers. We had trained the Russian volunteer chaplain in LOGOS teaching methods and he had been directing a Russian Reform School LOGOS Program for several months. The change in the boys' attitudes was remarkable.

After that experience in Russia, I wanted to find a place where LOGOS could be tried in an American youth prison. On September 15, 1998, a LOGOS Program was initiated at the New Mexico Boys' Reform School in Springer, New Mexico. Sixteen boys, chosen by counselors and prison staff, were invited to participate. The boys had to agree to attend worship each week to continue in the LOGOS Program. The chaplain and his LOGOS Director and staff worked very hard ministering to the boys. And added assistance came from The American Bible Society and *Guideposts Magazine,* who donated Bibles and magazines for the boys. All in all, the program was successful.

Any youth detention center or reform school around the country could have a similar program. If you know of a detention center in your area that may be interested in LOGOS, please contact me. Perhaps we can find caring members of congregations in your community that would be interested in reaching out and ministering to the youth.

Founding of the Wings Ministry

Nothing we do changes the past, but everything we do changes the future. Every person is responsible for building the future, planting for the next generation. What are we leaving to the children of our time?
                                        —Beechacres

During the years that I stayed home with my baby and

volunteered at the church, I began writing this book in order to help others struggling in a similar situation. By 1995, Dr. Poling, who had been following my progress, became very interested in my book and felt I should present a draft to the New Mexico Prison Fellowship Director in hopes of securing a publisher. The director did not seem interested in the book; however, he introduced me to the Angel Tree Program. Prison Fellowship sponsors the Angel Tree Program, wherein church members from multiple denominations across the United States are asked to buy Christmas presents for children of inmates. Each year, approximately 500,000 children receive Christmas presents on behalf of an inmate through this program. As I learned about the Angel Tree Program, I was reminded of the LOGOS Program, and I wondered if the two programs could compliment each other.

It seemed as if destiny was knocking at my door, because in the summer of 1995, a mission trip brought me through Washington, D.C., where Prison Fellowship happened to be holding its international conference. My associates and I were able to meet with the Vice President of the Angel Tree Program, as well as several other top leaders and area directors with Prison Fellowship. After explaining the LOGOS Program and how we felt it could be united with the Angel Tree Program, I was given a small grant to start the Wings Ministry.

I envisioned the Wings Ministry as a program wherein caring individuals could reach out and support the children and family members of inmates, helping them out of their "arrest" and showing them renewed life through Christ. It is heartwarming to know the "wings" of the volunteers serve to create a protective and safe haven for children and spouses of inmates.

Wings Model
The goal of the Wings Ministry is to connect the families

of inmates to caring youth and adults from churches in the local area. We strive to bring those lacking spiritual community into the activities of a church congregation. The Wings Ministry offers three parties a year: Christmas, Easter, and Back-To-School. These parties are based on the LOGOS format and provide the opportunity for church volunteers to develop Christian relationships with the families of inmates. The Wings parties use the LOGOS model of nurturing by building Christian relationships in a four part experience. Youth and adults from participating congregations in the community partner with the inmate's families to sing, take part in an interactive Bible study, share a meal together, and participate in recreational events.

During the activity time, the guardians and caregivers of the inmate's children have time to meet with church leaders, prison volunteers, LOGOS Associates, and Prison Fellowship representatives. Contacts can be made that will enable future support for these families. Invitations are extended to the families to attend worship services of congregations in their neighborhoods, and the inmate's families are encouraged to find a church home.

LOGOS: Special Projects Director

Prior to stepping up to the position of Special Projects Director, I had been actively involved as a LOGOS National Board Member for several years. I had been part of the Russian Ministry as an Assistant Group Leader on Adult and Youth Trips to Russia. Then I started the Wings Ministry that was based on the LOGOS Program. And, in the fall of 1995, Dr. Dale K. Milligan offered me a position to work full time for LOGOS.

For the next five years, I was very blessed to be a part of the LOGOS National Staff. LOGOS holds training schools all over the country and I was part of many training teams along with other dedicated pastors and lay leaders. I also taught Introductory Seminars in many churches and represented

LOGOS at National Conventions. As well as heading up Special Projects, which included the Wings Ministry, I helped organize the missions to Russia, and helped facilitate a new outreach program to India. Moreover, I coordinated regional and national LOGOS staff meetings and conventions and worked with Search Institute.

LOGOS in India

After the August 1995 discussions with Prison Fellowship and Angel Tree officials in Washington, D.C., Rev. Randall Webb and I explored the exhibits at the Prison Fellowship conference. When we came across the booth representing India, we met Prison Fellowship representative, Dr. Kunjaman Chaco, the founder of The Children's Home, an orphanage for children of prisoners. We shared our concern for children of prisoners and discussed our recent trip to Russia, where our team taught the LOGOS Program to Russian Orthodox leaders.

Dr. Chaco became so interested in the LOGOS Program that he invited us to visit India. He wanted us to teach pastors and church leaders how to implement the LOGOS Program. Subsequently, four LOGOS leaders, including myself, led the first LOGOS Training School in India. About one hundred and fifty pastors and lay leaders attended the four day training school. We also traveled to seven other cities in India, sharing information about LOGOS and building relationships for future training opportunities. We were welcomed all over the country, and those in attendance at the LOGOS Training School were energized by the LOGOS methods.

Search Institute

Under my responsibility of organizing special projects, I gained particular interest in Search Institute, an organization based in Minneapolis, MN. Dr. Peter Benson, President of Search Institute, was fundamental in identifying the "40 Developmental Assets" that all people need. Utilizing Dr. Benson's research, Search Institute established a method of testing teenagers which correlates the amount of positive "assets" they have in their lives with the amount of "at-risk behavior" they are likely to exhibit. Their testing proves that the more assets young people have, the less likely they are to get into trouble.

Search Institute has tested almost two million students across the U.S., and, unfortunately, has not found any community in which the youth are not at risk. The fundamental problem in teens' lives has been identified as a "depletion of assets." The good news, however, is that there is hope in the form of a solution. America's Promise, which was originally coordinated by Colin Powell and supported by all of America's living Presidents, has used Search Institute's research as part of the basis for their initiative.

LOGOS Associates quickly identified that the research that Search Institute was performing was vital for LOGOS' continued work with congregations. The LOGOS Program has a proven track record for building quality relationships between church members and their youth in order to establish strong moral values in teenagers. The LOGOS Program, when modeled correctly, can build at least thirty of the forty assets that Search Institute identifies. After contact was made by LOGOS Associates with Search Institute, I was able to build relationships with the leaders at Search Institute through the UCYD Project and the Wings Ministry.

Uniting Congregations for Youth Development (UCYD)

UCYD was a pilot project of Search Institute that sought

to equip congregations of all faiths with the tools to build developmental assets in young people. Seven cities in the United States were picked as pilot sites for a UCYD study. My place of residence, Albuquerque, New Mexico, was chosen as one of the seven sites, which presented an opportunity for me to become actively involved in the UCYD study. Through this research, and in accordance with my Wings involvement, I learned that children of prisoners are the most "at-risk" youth in America today. Therefore, I believe the "40 Developmental Assets" are as fundamental to adults as they are to children.

National Crime Statistics:

• Children of incarcerated family members are six times more likely to end up in prison.

• Approximately 75% of all female prisoners and 66% of all male prisoners are parents.

• Over 2 million children in the U.S. have a parent in prison.

• More than 50% of children of prisoners do not visit their incarcerated parent.

• Over 6.6 million Americans are either incarcerated or on probation/parole.

• 33% of African-American men in their twenties are incarcerated or on probation.

• Prison population has more than doubled in the past ten years.

• American recidivism, or prisoner return rate, is approximately 75%.

• Over $30 billion a year is spent to incarcerate America's prisoners.

For organizations, schools, congregations, and employers across the United States, Search Institute is addressing the importance of developing as many of the "assets" in young people as possible.

Americana Publishing, Inc.

In February, 2000, my friend, former pastor, and mentor, Dr. David Poling, introduced me to his business partner, George Lovato, Jr., CEO and Founder of Americana Publishing, Inc. Mr. Lovato was financially independent, making him a good candidate to donate funds to the LOGOS and Wings Ministry. However, when I met with Mr. Lovato and Dr. Poling, they offered me a sales position with their publishing firm. In addition, Dr. Poling mentioned my book to Mr. Lovato and he expressed interest in publishing it. I was overcome with gratitude, because I had spent many unsuccessful years searching for a publisher. However, accepting a new job meant leaving the LOGOS position that I cherished. Unfortunately, my jobs with not-for-profit organizations over the past twelve years had kept me at the poverty level, and I was tired of struggling financially. On the other hand, I was afraid that the IRS would garnish any income over $30,000. Therefore, before I ventured into a new job, I turned to the IRS one more time for a solution to my dilemma.

Innocent Spouse Relief

After waiting in line with my ticket, such as one would do

at a deli, I faced a woman who peered through her security window at me in shock. She informed me that I had a lot of nerve to walk into the IRS office knowing that I owed $30,000. I told her that she must have her information confused with someone else's records. She proceeded to enter more information into her computer; and, after a sudden gasp, she informed me that I owed over $3.5 million to the IRS. I responded by telling her that dollar figure seemed more accurate. For an hour I stood at her window and explained my story. By the grace of God, she happened to be the Innocent Spouse Relief expert for the entire state. Throughout my story, I told her that IRS agents had informed me that my last lien would never go away; rather, they would simply keep renewing it every ten years for the rest of my life. In fact, one agent told me that after I was dead he would attach the liens to my boys. She told me that those statements were untrue. Additionally, she clarified other untrue statements. I was able to earn over $30,000 without having it all garnished, and I was able to make a mistake on my tax return without being hauled into prison. Moreover, she explained that the IRS could not take my four boys away from me, as one IRS agent had threatened.

Upon explaining that I had filed an Innocent Spouse Relief Form six months earlier, she called for her director to assist us. She told me that all Innocent Spouse Relief cases had been put on hold due to the time of year and the huge number of claims. However, she was so shocked by my story and alarmed by all the lies I had been told over the years that she promised to pull my file and put it on the top of the list. She also promised to assign an agent to my case immediately, which she did. To my relief, the newly assigned IRS agent reviewed my case and recommended Innocent Spouse Relief in order to erase the entire debt.

Finally, a fifteen year burden had been lifted off my shoulders and I was free to pursue a career. I rejoiced and thanked God for the goodness that lies in the hearts of all the people that helped me through my struggle!

My Faith Journey

I have shared my personal story as an offering of hope. My journey has given me the opportunity to write this book, and opportunities will present themselves to you too. Try to keep a clear mind to see if the Holy Spirit is guiding you. I believe God presents himself to us in many forms. Sometimes God speaks to us through dreams and intuition; sometimes God speaks to us through others. Therefore, I encourage you to find a faith community where you can surround yourself with other caring people who love and appreciate you. Pray for guidance. Put your busy life on hold long enough to listen for God's words and direction. If I had not had my mentor and friend, Dr. Poling, this book would never have been completed nor published. He welcomed me into the church, he supported my writing, and he opened the door to my new job.

Look around you. Who believes in you and encourages you? Who is your mentor? What kind of relationship do you have with God? I promise you that with faith, support from loved ones, and prayer, you will find success. God bless you!

Untitled

Come and live a dream with me,
I shall give you the key.
You can be free—
no worries, no lies,
just you and me.
Please promise me
that you will share the key,
so everyone can live the dream
with you and me.

—Ann Edenfield's son, age 16

25 Phrases
of Affirmation and Love

1.   I love you.

2.   You're doing beautifully.

3.   It's a pleasure to teach you.

4.   Good thinking.

5.   I'm proud of the job you've done.

6.   You're special.

7.   You make me happy.

8.   I enjoy being with you.

9.   You remembered.

10.   Keep up the good work.

11.   You're very good at that.

12.   I knew you could do it.

13.   That's quite an improvement.

14.   You're learning quickly.

15.   You're getting better every day.

16.   That's the best yet.

17.   You're really improving.

18.   You did very well.

19.   You make me happy.

20.   I couldn't have done it better.

21.   You outdid yourself.

22.   Way to go.

23.   One more time and you'll have it.

24.   You've been practicing.

25.   Good job.

40 Developmental Assets

Search Institute has identified the following building blocks of healthy development that help young people grow up healthy, caring, and responsible.

External Assets

Category   **Asset Name and Definition**

Support

1. **Family Support** Family life provides high levels of love and support.
2. **Positive Family Communication** Young person and her or his parent(s) communicate positively, and young person is willing to seek advice and counsel from parents.
3. **Other Adult Relationships** Young person perceives that adults in the community value youth.
4. **Caring Neighborhood** Young person experiences caring neighbors.
5. **Caring School Climate** School provides a caring, encouraging environment.
6. **Parent Involvement in Schooling** Parent(s) are actively involved in helping young person succeed in school.

Empowerment

7. **Community Values Youth** Young person perceives that adults in the community value youth.

8. **Youth as Resources** Young people are given useful roles in the community.

9. **Service to Others** Young person serves in the community one hour or more per week.

10. **Safety** Young person feels safe at home, school, and in the neighborhood.

Boundaries and Expectations

11. **Family Boundaries** Family has clear rules and consequences and monitors the young person's whereabouts.

12. **School Boundaries** School provides clear rules and consequences.

13. **Neighborhood Boundaries** Neighbors take responsibility for monitoring young people's behavior.

14. **Adult Role Models** Parent(s) and other adult's model positive, responsible behavior.

15. **Positive Peer Influence** Young person's best friends model responsible behavior.

16. **High Expectations** Both parent(s) and teachers encourage the young person to do well.

Constructive Use of Time

17. **Creative Activities** Young person spends three or more hours per week in lessons or practice in music, theatre, or other arts.

18. **Youth programs** Young person spends three or more hours per week in sports, clubs, or organizations at school and/or in the community.

19. **Religious Community** Young person spends one or more

hours per week in activities in a religious institution.

20. **Time at Home** Young person is out with friends "with nothing special to do" two or fewer nights per week.

Internal Assets

Category　　　**Asset Name and Definition**

Commitment to Learning

21. **Achievement Motivation** Young person is motivated to do well in school.

22. **School Engagement** Young person is actively engaged in learning.

23. **Homework** Young person reports doing at least one hour of homework every school day.

24. **Bonding to School** Young person cares about her or his school.

25. **Reading for Pleasure** Young person reads for pleasure three or more hours per week.

Positive Values

26. **Caring** Young person places high value on helping other people.

27. **Equality and Social Justice** Young person places high value on promoting equality and reducing hunger and poverty.

28. **Integrity** Young person acts on convictions and stands up for her or his beliefs.

29. **Honesty** Young person "tells the truth even when it is not easy."

30. **Responsibility** Young person accepts and takes personal

responsibility.

31. **Restraint** Young person believes it is important not to be sexually active or to use alcohol or other drugs.

Social Competencies

32. **Planning and Decision Making** Young person knows how to plan ahead and make choices.

33. **Interpersonal Competence** Young person has empathy, sensitivity, and friendship skills.

34. **Cultural Competence** Young person has knowledge of and comfort with people of different cultural/racial/ethnic backgrounds.

35. **Resistance Skills** Young person can resist negative peer pressure and dangerous situations.

36. **Peaceful Conflict Resolution** Young person seeks to resolve conflict nonviolently.

Positive Identity

37. **Personal Power** Young person feels he or she has control over "things that happen to me."

38. **Self-Esteem** Young person reports having a high self-esteem.

39. **Sense of Purpose** Young person reports that "my life has a purpose."

40. **Positive View of Personal Future** Young person is optimistic about her or his personal future.

Legal Terms

Ab Initio
From the beginning

Ad Hoc
For this; for a particular purpose

Ante
Before; previous part

Axiom
A universal truth

Chattel
A moveable item of personal property

Coram Vobis
Before you; in your presence

Corpus Delicti
The body of the crime or the victim

De Facto
In fact

Et Al
And others

Ex post Facto
After the fact

Exculpatory
Clearing or tending to clear from alleged fault or guilt

MR
Mandatory Release; the date the prisoner will be released with consideration for all good time, no disciplinary problems, and no parole

Security Operations Ranking
for Adult Correctional Facilities

Warden
Chief Operating Officer

Deputy Warden of Operations
Assists the Warden and usually oversees security

Chief of Security
Oversees security and supervises the Captain(s) under his command (usually a Major)

Captain
Administrator that supervises the Lieutenant(s) under his command

Lieutenant
Supervises basic operations of the prison

Sergeant
Available to assist and supervise correctional officers

Correctional Officer
Oversees the inmates

Toll Free Telephone Numbers
Motels & Hotels in the United States

Best Western	1-800-528-1234
Courtyard	1-800-321-2211
Days Inn	1-800-325-2525
Doubletree	1-800-528-0444
Drury Inns	1-800-325-8300
Embassy Suites	1-800-362-2779
Exel Inns	1-800-356-8013
Friendship Inns International	1-800-453-4511
Four Seasons	1-800-332-3442
Guest Quarters	1-800-424-2900
Hampton Inns	1-800-426-7866
Harley Hotels	1-800-321-2323
Hilton Hotels	1-800-445-8667
Holiday Inn	1-800-465-4329
Homewood Suites	1-800-225-5466
Howard Johnson	1-800-654-2000
Hyatt Hotels	1-800-228-9000
Intercontinental	1-800-327-0200
Marriott	1-800-228-9290
Motel 6	1-800-466-8356
Omni International	1-800-843-6664
Quality Inn	1-800-228-5151
Radisson	1-800-333-3333
Ramada Inn	1-800-228-2828
Red Lion Hotels & Inns	1-800-547-8010

Red Roof	1-800-843-7663
Residence Inn	1-800-331-3131
Rodeway	1-800-228-2000
Sheraton	1-800-325-3535
Stouffer	1-800-468-3571
Super 8 Motels	1-800-800-8000
General Assistance	1-800-555-1212

Organizations and Services

AIDS Hotline
1-800-545-2437

Alcoholics Anonymous
A.A. World Services, Inc.
P.O Box 459
New York, NY 10163
1-212-870-3400
http://www.alcoholics-anonymous.org
Headquarters:
Alcoholics Anonymous
475 Riverside Drive - 11th Floor
New York, NY 10115

American Bar Association
1-800-215-1190
http://www.getareferral.com

American Bible Association
1865 Broadway
New York, NY 10023
1-212-408-1200
1-800-32-BIBLE (For scripture inquiries)
http://www.americanbible.org

American Correctional Association
4380 Forbes Boulevard
Lanham, MD   20706-4322
ph 1-800-222-5646   fax 1-301-918-1900
http://www.aca.org

Angel Tree Program of Prison Fellowship
PO Box 17500
Washington, DC 20041
1-800-55-ANGEL
http://www.angeltree.org

Domestic Violence National Hotline
1-800-799-7233 (General Information)

Family and Corrections Network
32 Oak Grove Road
Palmyra, VA 22963
ph 1-434-589-3036   fax 434-589-6520
http://www.fcnetwork.org

Families Against Mandatory Minimums (FAMM)
1612 K St., N.W., Suite 1400
Washington, D.C. 20006
ph 1-202- 822-6700 fax 1-202- 822-6704
http://www.famm.org

Federal Bonding Program
1-800-233-2258
Department of Labor at 1-877-US2JOBS
http://www.bonds4jobs.com
http://www.usworkforce.org/onestop

Federal Bureau of Prisons
320 First St. NW
Washington, DC 20534
1-202-307-3198
http://www.bop.gov
http://www.unicor.gov

Focus on the Family
8605 Explorer Drive
Colorado Spring, CO 80920
ph 1-800-A-FAMILY or 1-800-232-6459   fax 1-719-548-4654
http://www.family.org

Global LOGOS, Inc.
504 Allen Road, Suite 100
Ferndale, MI 48220-2445
http://www.GlobalLOGOS.org

Guideposts Magazine
39 Seminary Hill Road
Carmel, NY 10512
ph 1-845-225-3681   fax 1-845-228-2115
http://www.guideposts.com

Hepatitis C - Treatment Information
http://www.veritasmedicine.com

LOGOS System Associates
1405 Frey Road
Pittsburgh, PA 15235
1-877-YES-2-LSA or 1-877-937-2572
http://www.logos-system.org

Martindale-Hubbell
http://www.lawyers.com

Narcotics Anonymous
World Service Office in Los Angeles
PO Box 9999
Van Nuys, California 91409 USA
ph 1-828-773-9999   fax 1-818-700-0700
http://www.na.org

National Criminal Justice Reference Service (NCJRS)
PO Box 6000
Rockville, MD 20849-6000
ph 1-800-851-3420   fax 1-410-792-4358
http://puborder.ncjrs.org

Prison Fellowship
PO Box 1550
Merrifield, VA 22116-1550
1-877-478-0100 Customer Service
ph 1-703-478-0100   fax 1-703-478-0452
http://www.pfm.org

Rape Abuse Incest National Network (RAINN)
635-B Pennsylvania Ave., SE
Washington, DC 20003
Counselor: 1-800-656-HOPE Ext. 1
Business Office: 1-800-656-HOPE x3   fax 1-202-544-3556
http://www.rainn.org

Red Cross
1-800-435-7669
http://www.redcross.org

Runaway Hotline (National)
1-800-621-4000
3880 North Lincoln Ave.
Chicago, IL 60657
http://www.nrscrisisline.org

Salvation Army
International Headquarters
101 Queen Victoria Street
London EC4P 4EP, United Kingdom
ph 020 7332 0101   fax 020 7236 4981
International:
ph [44] 20 7332 0101   fax [44] 20 7236 4981
http://salvationarmy.org

Search Institute
The Banks Building
615 First Avenue NE, Suite 125
Minneapolis, MN 55413
1-800-888-7828
ph 1-612-376-8955   fax 1-612-376-8956
http://www.search-institute.org

Social Security Administration
1-800-772-1213

Suicide Hotline
1-800-SUICIDE
1-800-784-2433   24 hours/7 days
http://www.SuicideHotlines.com

U.S. Department of Health and Human Services
370 L'Enfant Promenade SW

Washington, DC 20447
http://www.adf.dhhs.gov

Child Abuse - Childhelp's National Child Abuse Hotline

1-800-4-A-CHILD (1-800-422-4453)

Child Care - Child Care Aware

1-800-424-2246

Domestic Violence - National Domestic Violence Hotline

1-800-799-SAFE (7233) 1-800-787-3224

Missing and Exploited Children

1-800-THE-LOST (1-800-843-5678)

Runaway Youth

1-800-621-4000

U.S. Department of Justice

Office of Justice Programs
Washington, DC 20531
http://www.ojp.usdoj.gov

Wings Ministry

2226 B Wyoming NE #130
Albuquerque, NM 87112
http://www.WingsMinistry.org
ph 1-505-291-6412 fax 1-505-291-6418

email: AnnEdenfield@WingsMinistry.org

Glossary
Vocabulary of the Prison and Judicial System

Administrative Procedures
Procedures that must be followed in a certain order when there is a remedy grievance. If proper order is not followed, the officials can and will deny relief to an inmate relief. An inmate starts with the lowest form, a cop out.

Attorney at Law/Lawyer/Counselor at Law
Person legally empowered to act as agent for, or on behalf of another, regarding the law

A/W
Associate Warden

Bail
Money or credit deposited with the court to get an arrested person temporarily released with the assurance that he will appear in court at the appointed time

Bond
Evidence of a debt that secures bail

BOP
Bureau of Prisons

Breathalyzer
Machine which tests alcohol level in a person's blood

Bring It All
Complete an entire prison sentence

Bunkie
Inmate who sleeps above or below an inmate in bunk beds and shares a cell or room

Captain
Head correctional officer

Case Worker
Prison staff member assigned to manage a prisoner's progress reports

CIMS
Central Inmate Monitoring System—determines an inmate's prison appointment and generally insures that two people convicted jointly in a crime will not be assigned to the same prison

Co-defendant
Two people acting jointly in a crime and charged with the same crime

Common Fare
Name given to a special diet, which an inmate adheres to for religious or medical reasons

Commissary
Retail shop within the confines of the prison where all purchases must be made through a commissary account

Computation Sheet
Document prepared by the state, region, or institution, which shows an inmate's release date and the amount of good time he is able to earn

Cop Out
Request written by an inmate

Contraband
Any item not listed on an inmate's inventory form. A prisoner is subject to disciplinary action if caught with contraband in his possession.

Correctional Officer
Prison guard

Counselor
Social worker or psychologist available to an inmate for counseling

Count
Total head count of the prison population

Cube or Condo
An inmate's cell

C.T.C
Community Treatment Center

Day Pass
Twelve hour visitation time with family outside of the prison

Dump-truck
Slang for an attorney who ignores an inmate once that inmate is incarcerated

Executive Assistant
Warden's assistant—liaison for press and community activities

Expiration
Completion date of the prison sentence

Extra Duty
Work assigned to an inmate as a disciplinary measure

Fall Partner
Person with whom a crime was committed

Furlough
Time granted to an inmate to leave the prison for a designated period of time

Good Conduct Time
Amount of time deducted from the back end of the sentence for good behavior

Folding money or currency
American dollars—considered contraband in prison

Grand Jury
Jury of 12 to 23 persons convened in private session to evaluate accusations against persons charged with crime and to determine whether the evidence warrants an indictment

Hack
Correctional officer

The Hole
Solitary confinement given as a disciplinary measure

Home Boy/Homey
A friend or fellow gangmember

Hooch
Beer or homemade liquor

How Short are You?
How much time do you have left to serve?

Indictment
Charge that must be proven at trial beyond a reasonable doubt in order to convict a defendant

In the Car
Inclusion in a group activity

Iron Pile
Weight room in the prison

Jacket
Criminal/prison record

Lieutenant
Supervises basic operations of the prison

LOGOS Program
The LOGOS Program is based on ACTS 2:42. "They devoted

themselves to the apostles' teaching and fellowship, to the breaking of bread and the prayers." Or, in LOGOS terms: Bible Study, Recreation, Worship Skills, and Meal Time. Greek word for "The Word" - as it says in the New Testament, John 1:1, "The Word was made flesh and dwelt among us." Jesus became the Word, and in the LOGOS Program, caring adults are taught how to relate, love, and nurture young people, so that the Word of God is also made known to them.

LOP
Low On Potential—someone inmates do not like or who has severe difficulty adjusting to prison life

Lump Sum Award
Special time awarded to an inmate for some type of special performance, which is subtracted from release date

M.R.
Mandatory Release—date an inmate will be released with consideration for all good time, no disciplinary problems, and no parole

N.O.A
Notice of Action—form the parole board uses to tell an inmate the date of his release

Number
State or federal number issued to an inmate for identification purposes that must be memorized by an inmate and should be recorded on all paperwork

Parole
Conditional, supervised release time following a prison term

Parole Board
Federal panel appointed by the Parole Commission in
Washington, D.C., which reviews an inmate's performance while
in prison and has the authority to establish a release date—each
state creates its own Parole Board and mandates its own policies

PMO
Postal Money Order—preferred type of funds for an inmate

Prison Levels
Minimum Security
Minimum Restrict
Medium Security
Maximum Security
Super Maximum Security

Progress Report
Record of an inmate's progress while in prison

P.S.I.
Pre-sentencing investigation regarding a defendant's character
and crime

Rack
Bunk bed

Road Dog
Friend in prison

Search Institute
Organization credited with identifying the "40 Developmental
Assets" of character and behavior

Shot
Disciplinary action; can range from extra duty to loss of good conduct time

Snitch
Inmate who reports inappropriate behavior of another inmate to prison officials

SPO
Special Purchase Order—form used to purchase items that need to be ordered from a source outside of the prison

UA
Urine Analysis—test that identifies the presence of drugs in an inmate.

UNICOR
Federal Prison Industries, Inc.—employs and provides skills training to the greatest practicable number of inmates

Unit Manager
Dorm supervisor—counselors and case managers work under the supervision of the unit manager

Warden
General Manager of a prison

Wings Ministry
Outreach program established for the spouses, children, and family members of prisoners

Index

A

AAA 87-88
Alcohol 25,34-36,69,77,117,140-141
Americana Publishing, Inc. 156
Angel Tree Program 151,153,172
Authorization Forms 109

B

Bail 10,12,15,18-19,27,34-35,177
Bond 17-21,35,177
Bureau of Prisons (BOP) 59,111,116,140-141,173

C

Central Inmate Monitoring System (CIMS) 178
Chain of Custody 118,120
Coins 107
Commissary 41-42,84,106-107,178
Condition of Release 17
Conjugal Visits 68
Contraband 77-78,107,179
Coupons 91-92

D

Dental Appointments 115

For more information
about the Wings Ministry visit:
www.WingsMinistry.org

or write to:
Wings Ministry
2226 B Wyoming NE #130
Albuquerque, NM 87112

email: AnnEdenfield@WingsMinistry.org

ORDER A COPY TODAY

FAMILY ARRESTED:

How To Survive The Incarceration Of A Loved One

Print Book: **$14.95** ISBN: 1-58943-060-3
Audio Book: **$22.00** ISBN: 1-58807-099-9 • 3 Tapes • Unabridged
Read by Ann Edenfield, Author

Ship To:

Name

Address

City/State/Zip

Phone   email address

— Check   — Money order   — Credit Card   — Visa   — MC

Credit Card#   Exp. Date

Name as it appears on card

Signature

Shipping & Handling: $5.00 (1-2 books) $1.00 shipping each additional book.

Print Book x **$14.95**	$ _____
Audio Book x **$22.00**	$ _____
Shipping/Handling x **$5.00**	$ _____
Shipping x **$1.00**	$ _____
Total Order Amount	$ _____

FOR ADDITIONAL ORDERS

Call Toll Free: 1-888-883-8203 x157   Fax: 1-505-255-6189
Mail To: Americana Publishing, Inc.
         303 San Mateo NE, Suite 104 A, Albuquerque, NM 87108